Hip Hollywood Homes

Hip Hollywood Homes

> An Intimate Look at L.A.'s Hottest Trendsetters and the Inspiring Spaces They Live In

Sue Hostetler

Foreword by > **Courteney Cox Arquette**
Interviews by > **Merle Ginsberg**
Photographs by > **Peter Christiansen Valli**

CLARKSON POTTER / PUBLISHERS

NEW YORK

Copyright © 2006 by Sue Hostetler
Photographs copyright © 2006 by Peter Christiansen Valli
Foreword copyright © 2006 by Courteney Cox Arquette

Published in the United States by Clarkson Potter/Publishers, an imprint of
the Crown Publishing Group, a division of Random House, Inc., New York.
www.crownpublishing.com
www.clarksonpotter.com

Clarkson N. Potter is a trademark and Potter and colophon are registered
trademarks of Random House, Inc.

Library of Congress Cataloging-in-Publication Data
Hostetler, Sue.
    Hip Hollywood homes / Sue Hostetler; foreword by Courteney Cox
Arquette; interviews by Merle Ginsberg; photographs by Peter Christiansen
Valli.—1st ed.   1. Architecture, Domestic—California—Los Angeles.   2.
Celebrities—Homes and haunt—California—Los Angeles.   3. Los Angeles
(Calif.)—Buildings, structures, etc.   4. Hollywood (Los Angeles, Calif.)—
Buildings, structures, etc.   I. Ginsberg, Merle.   II. Valli, Peter Christiansen.
III. Title.
NA7238.L6H67   2006
728'.370979494—dc22   2005030735

ISBN-13: 978-0-307-23826-9
ISBN-10: 0-307-23826-1

Printed in China

Design by Maureen Erbe, Rita Sowins / Erbe Design

Additional interviews by Julie La'Bassiere

10 9 8 7 6 5 4 3 2 1

First Edition

Photography Credits

Courtesy of John Ellis	24
Richard Neutra Miller residence © J. Paul Getty Trust. Used with permission. Julius Shulman Photography Archive Research Library at the Getty Research Institute (2004.R.10)	64
Portrait courtesy of Dewey Nicks	79
Will and Ariel Durant residence. Courtesy of Monica Ariel Mihell	105
Rudolf Schindler Elliot residence © J. Paul Getty Trust. Used with permission. Julius Shulman Photography Archive Research Library at the Getty Research Institute (2004.R.10)	141
Wallace Neff Myrtle A. Horenstein residence. Courtesy of the Maynard Parker Collection and the Huntington Library	167

Acknowledgments

Sincere thanks and a debt of gratitude are due to many people, without whom this book would not have been possible. A project of this magnitude is a collaborative effort, so a very heartfelt thank-you goes to Peter Christiansen Valli for his gorgeous, inspiring photography and commitment; Merle Ginsberg for her support and friendship; and Julie La'Bassiere for help in the final hours. A special thanks to Courteney Cox Arquette for contributing her insightful words and thoughts about life in Los Angeles.

Thank you to the team at Clarkson Potter for their faith and guidance, including my brilliant editor, Aliza Fogelson, publisher Lauren Shakely, Pam Krauss, Marysarah Quinn, Jane Treuhaft, Maureen Erbe, Rita Sowins, Mark McCauslin, Felix Gregorio, Maria Gagliano, and Chris Pavone, for getting it all started.

Special thanks to Peter Valli's hardworking and comical assistants, Glen and Melissa.

My genuine appreciation for wise advice and terrific ideas goes to Carol Irish and Isabel Venero. Additional thanks to: Vanessa King, Dewey Nicks, John Ellis, Cynthia Pett-Dante, Alletta Kriak, Jill Eisenstadt, Susan Campos, Julie Taylor, Tonya Toone, Amy Licata, Maggie Haynes, Josh Rothstein, Timothy Woolston, Britany Lindgren, Amy Zvi, Amanda Gruder Rothman, Monica Mihell, the Getty Research Institute, and the Huntington Library.

And a most important thank you to my inspirations in love and life, Jon and Spencer.

Finally, to the real stars of the show—the people. I admire and respect the L.A. residents profiled here, what they do, and how they live; and I very much appreciate their participation. They are the coolest of the cool and I feel lucky to have spent time with them in their hip homes.

Contents

Hollywood is diverse. It is complex. It is unpredictable. Almost every culture in the world is represented somewhere in the city. Hollywood is glamorous and ordinary, cutting-edge and refined. Just like the people who live here, Hollywood homes reflect a creativity and sensibility that is rarely seen elsewhere. Styles converge and sometimes collide with often unexpected results. With *Hip Hollywood Homes,* Sue Hostetler has given us a chance to peek inside some of the most uniquely designed residences in Los Angeles. Enjoy.

—Courteney Cox Arquette

Los Angeles. The name evokes so many familiar images: clear blue skies, majestic palm trees, warm sunshine, glistening swimming pools, magnificent tanned bodies, gleaming sports cars, elegant Rodeo Drive boutiques, star-studded Hollywood parties, groovy nightclubs on the Sunset Strip, and sparkling Malibu beaches. We all know these popular sights by heart, through the Academy Awards, magazine spreads, and infotainment shows. They are the instantly recognizable shorthand symbols of Los Angeles. Yet they barely scratch the surface of what I have come to know as the authentic Los Angeles, or "Angeleno," style. Beyond the glitz and glamour of Hollywood, true L.A. style stems from a state of mind—one of freedom, individuality, and life-affirming optimism—that can be expressed in so many different ways, from minimalist West Coast cool to over-the-top exoticism.

When I started living part-time in Los Angeles a few years ago, I was immediately struck by two things: the people and the way they live here. The kind of life one can lead and the variety of homes one can have in Los Angeles is like nowhere else in the world. In a city of seemingly unending space and light, creativity and imagination know no limits. I soon realized that what was so unique about L.A. style was the potent mix of cultural influences and indigenous terrain: spectacular confluences of Spanish, French, Italian, Asian, Moroccan, and other far-flung traditions set against wildly varied sun-drenched backdrops of beach, mountains, and desert. All of these combine to form America's most original indoor and outdoor architecture and decor.

But it was also the people who amazed me. I felt an unbelievable creative electricity among friends and colleagues: a cultural renaissance was taking place, and it appeared that Los Angeles was fast becoming the epicenter for hip creative genius in the twenty-first century. These individuals—strong-minded trailblazers and uninhibited risk takers—were changing the face of fashion, music, art, design, entertainment, publishing, and film. I was in awe, and I wanted to know exactly what inspired this group of pioneering tastemakers and how each of them had interpreted L.A. style for their own private homes.

Southern California Architecture

For nearly a century, Los Angeles has been the incubator for some of the country's most exciting architectural trends: from historical revival styles, including English Arts and Crafts, Spanish Revival, French Norman and Colonial Revival, to Modernism, California Ranch, and a whole array of more contemporary styles. Like the homesteading pioneers before them, the design greats must have initially been drawn to California by the wide, open spaces and rich agricultural land. The mild climate undoubtedly inspired the unique design relationship between indoors and out, while a cluster of prestigious architectural schools that celebrated excellence in residential design was surely another attraction. And maybe there was the added lure of a new magazine called *Arts and Architecture* and the creation of the Case Study House Program.

Whatever the draw, L.A. architects have embraced an incredible range of styles over the years. A look back illustrates just how innovative, versatile, and visionary California architecture and design have been and continue to be: from the 1920s and the glass structure with outdoor sleeping porches of Richard Neutra's Lovell House (featured in the movie *L.A. Confidential*); to the 1930s and the grand stone Georgian Revival Kirkeby Mansion in Bel Air, built by Chicago hotel magnate Arnold Kirkeby (made famous by *The Beverly Hillbillies*); to the 1950s and Pierre Koenig's Case Study House No. 22, immortalized in that iconic photograph by Julius Shulman; to the 1960s and '70s when Tony Duquette designed and redesigned his famed Beverly Hills estate Dawnridge, ornately decorated and situated in a jaw-dropping garden full of pagodas, footbridges, terraces, obelisks, and pavilions, all on multiple levels; to the present day and Peter Morton's recently completed two-story teak and concrete Malibu residence, unlike anything ever designed by genius Richard Meier.

Very often L.A. homes have been the result of a spirited collaboration between architects and movie-star patrons seeking to create the ultimate Hollywood fantasy homes. From the 1920s through the '50s, Wallace Neff, touted as the "architect of California's golden age," built homes for the likes of Charlie Chaplin, Groucho Marx, Cary Grant, and Fredric March. His renovation of the renowned English Tudor–style Pickfair for Mary Pickford and Douglas Fairbanks was immediately dubbed Hollywood's "White House." Today many celebrities are still disciples: when they were married, Brad Pitt and Jennifer Aniston bought March's former Beverly Hills Neff home and added a Frank Gehry–designed wine cellar (followed by rumors of Pitt and Gehry working on something together); Diane Keaton renovated a 1928 Art Deco house designed by Frank Lloyd Wright; and to inaugurate a new L.A.-based chapter in his life, fashion designer Tom Ford bought and refurbished, with the help of the great preservationist firm Marmol Radziner, one of Neutra's finest residences. Most important, this relatively new obsession among stylish residents to find and lovingly restore modern homes by the legendary mid-century architects, is done with a meticulous eye and keen understanding of the original design, the architectural context and legacy of the property.

A New Breed of Interior Designer

All of the residences profiled in *Hip Hollywood Homes* have historical roots, but the truly amazing thing is how their current owners—sometimes in collaboration with interior designers—have created spaces with so much fresh, individual style. These incredible style-conscious inhabitants are true originals who, instead of following some tired design formula or fad, are rewriting how they want to live according to their personal vision, taste, passion, and whim.

A new breed of interior designer who refuses to accept the norm is making Los Angeles a more visually stimulating and fulfilling place to live. Tim Andreas is bringing the same concepts—sleek, chic with a dash of quirky—to the private homes of Angelenos that he helped pioneer as design director at Ian Schrager's hotels. Brad Dunning has become the designer for L.A. residents with strong tastes and bold ideas. He has transformed an office originally designed by Irving Gill for photographer Dewey

Nicks and created homes, known for their inventiveness and quality, for agent Bryan Lourd and director Sofia Coppola. There is the unconventional yet timeless work of Valerie Pasquiou, who expertly blended pieces from various periods for literary agent Bob Bookman's reinvention of Howard Hughes and Katharine Hepburn's former home. Tim Clark, Brenda Antin, Kishani Perera—the list of designers turning convention on its ear and changing the contemporary landscape of L.A. interior design goes on and on.

The People

Hip Hollywood Homes takes you behind the scenes with some of the most influential and well, yes, hip residents in Los Angeles. Everyone may have a different idea of what that all-American word means, but no one can dispute that it applies to L.A. style makers like Pamela Skaist-Levy, who has altered the way that women around the world dress with Juicy Couture; Darren Star and Ryan Murphy, who have changed our expectations of television and pushed the limits with *Sex and the City* and *nip/tuck,* respectively; Shaun Caley Regen, who is educating us about great contemporary art; or Jason Binn, who has changed the face of magazine publishing in several of the most important U.S. cities. And though everyone profiled is incredibly successful, really enjoying life seems to be their secret for being and staying happy.

My Idea of L.A. Style

I love L.A. I love the whole vibe of Jeff Klein's Argyle Hotel, where John Wayne once lived with his cow and which has been newly remodeled by the great Paul Fortune. I love popping into Tracey Ross in Sunset Plaza to have Tracey or Karen outfit me for the night. I love the narrow leafy streets that curve up the hills of Los Feliz and looking up to see Frank Lloyd Wright's monumental brick Ennis-Brown House. I love the way that all the surfer girls wear their Uggs into Nobu Malibu. I love eating pasta on the patio at Orso with friends and watching all of the paparazzi across the street while having lunch at the Ivy. I love zooming down Wilshire by the I. M. Pei–designed CAA building where you can spot the agents—the only men in Los Angeles wearing suits. I love mingling at Hollyhock during one of Suzanne Rheinstein's elegant book parties. I love watching the musclemen pump iron on the beach in Venice. I love hunting through the funky little shops in Silverlake for that perfect gift. I love all of the valets, in their tennis shirts at the Beverly Hills Hotel, who park my car when I breeze in for cocktails at the Polo Lounge. I love taking the PCH all the way out to Point Dume on the weekends with bread to feed the seagulls with Spencer and Jon. I love flying into Burbank airport, driving over the hill, and being in West Hollywood in fifteen minutes. I love that I can wear jeans on almost any evening out in Los Angeles and feel dressed up. I love rockin' out at parties by the pool at Amanda Demme's bar in the Roosevelt Hotel. I love all of the newsstands that dot the city and actually carry the *New York Post.* I love the "Masters of Architecture" lecture series at the Los Angeles County Museum of Art, where you can hear everyone from Helmut Jahn to Rafael Viñoly speak. I love slipping into Decades on Melrose to search for secondhand Saint Laurent and sneaking next door to find first-edition books at Dailey's. I love imagining another era while looking at the stately homes in Hancock Park. I love that Joan's on Third operates on the honor system for payment. I love that the Getty doesn't treat photography as a second-class art. I love L.A.

Ready for Its Closeup

The creativity, glamour, and individuality of the residents, the year-round greenery and beauty, and the diversity and inspiration of the local architecture and design all make L.A. life incomparable. With the collision of rock 'n' roll and jazz, surfing and skateboarding, denim and diamonds influencing L.A. culture, hip is in every corner, every cool little boutique, and every peace-marked car in this city. There is no place else that looks like this: diverse yet cohesive, individualistic yet still amazingly unified. And no other city lives like this: indoors and outdoors, incorporating fire, water, sea, and sky in equal measures, offering unlimited lifestyle possibilities.

This book seeks to capture the spirit of the city and its people, while paying tribute to the historical, architectural, and stylistic influences behind it all. I am lucky enough to be friends with some of the people I profile here—people who create, shape, and embody everything that is L.A. style. Enjoy this intimate peek inside their rarely seen private lives and homes. This is a city where the real action happens behind beautifully designed but often closed doors.

Welcome to L.A.

—Sue Hostetler

Somewhere in a seemingly impossible, seemingly imaginary L.A. crossroads between Parisian haute couture, New York's fashion magazine elite, Hollywood's social scene, and a very strong sense of old-world family sits Jacqui Coppola Getty, whom many consider to live at the intersection of Hollywood and Style. And her house on a hill in Whitley Heights, which she's lived in for fifteen years, is style's temple—with a big dash of normality and reality thrown in.

It would be hard to find another woman in the Hollywood Hills cooking a rustic pasta meal for her husband of six years, Peter Getty, and her eighteen-year-old daughter, Gia Coppola, while wearing a combo of Lanvin and Balenciaga, purchased in both labels' Parisian boutiques. You might find the pasta (although carbs, particularly homemade ones, are hard to come by in Los Angeles), but you'd never get the Lanvin with it. Jacqui is dressed this way for a reason: designer Zac Posen is nipping into town for a night, and she's his Hollywood *guide de nuit*. There's no time to change. And she loves great clothes, anyway. No wonder all designers adore her.

"I guess people started acknowledging me as a fashion person when I began hosting some fashion parties in town," she says, grabbing a glass of Coppola cabernet in her cozy kitchen, in the midst of stirring. On her fridge are outtakes from a photo shoot she just did with Lanvin's Alber Elbaz for *Harper's Bazaar,* where she's a contributing editor. Before that, she was a costume designer on movies and music videos (to some very groovy bands like the Strokes, Green Day, etc.), an L.A.-based stylist, and a hostess with the mostest wardrobe, who would always have the newest Tom Ford–designed Gucci and YSL seasons ahead of the same celebrities she'd be partying with.

"I love clothes, I love designers, and I feel like fashion is a piece of art. And I collect it like it's art. I appreciate shapes and fabrics, particularly after years of shooting music videos and now shooting for *Bazaar*. I've learned a lot from Glenda Bailey [editor-in-chief of *Harper's Bazaar*], and from my friendship with Demi Moore, collaborating on dressing her for some things. Tom Ford knows how to make a woman look sexy. Alber makes women feel charming. Balenciaga is just genius. I'm a cheerleader for whatever designers I believe in. They're artists. I love the history of it all."

And a famous fashion face is responsible for the unique spelling of her name. Starting a tour of the two-story house, she shows off a collection of first-edition fashion, history, and photography books in her bedroom. Among the animal prints, fur blanket, and collection of coral is a Richard Avedon first edition. The famed fashion photographer gave it to her as a gift when she worked with him on a shoot on the set of *The Godfather, Part 3* (directed by Francis Ford Coppola—Gia's dad is his late son, Giancarlo). "Avedon signed the book and he spelled my name 'Jacqui.' And I've been spelling it that way ever since." (It was formerly "Jackie.") While the bedroom also includes chamois-colored suede-backed chairs from the forties, Hermès ashtrays, and a little black marble table, it's clearly the Avedon signature that represents Getty's style the most. Everything she owns is stylish but at the same time personal—and quirkily presented in a singular way.

Getty predecessor and fashion muse the late Talitha Getty (her hippie chic was renowned long before the term ever existed) is another fashion icon of Jacqui's. "She was beautiful," Getty says. "She was free, wild, and wore caftans—but I don't think she was trying to be a fashion icon. She just loved caftans—which I do, too. I was obsessed with her even before I married Peter."

Fifteen years ago, Jacqui and her daughter, Gia—who'd lived in both Napa Valley and in Rome for a year when Francis Coppola was directing *The Godfather, Part 3*—moved down to Los Angeles, into a West Hollywood duplex in the flats. "Francis decided the kids needed a real home, and a friend of ours, Laurie Frank, lived up here and told us there was a house about to go on the market. The house was built in 1922, but the backyard was all cement, the kitchen was three tiny rooms, and the whole vibe was very seventies—seventies paneling, sconces. I was *not* into the seventies; I wanted to get rid of that and restore it to its original state. I had fifteen thousand dollars to do the kitchen—and I just figured out what would be inexpensive and knocked out some walls. I did love the fact that my daughter's bedroom would be next to mine and that there was a little bedroom for a nanny. I was doing night shoots then. Then we tore the cement out of the garage, and everything came together."

Turned out the Whitley Heights house had its own history: situated near the early Hollywood studios of the twenties, Whitley was home to Rudolph Valentino, Jean Harlow, Maurice Chevalier, and a bevy of starlets who came and went.

Jacqui's role as home entertaining queen happened quite organically, as she was a single mom with a child, and didn't want to get a babysitter. Roman Coppola bought a house nearby in Whitley, and eventually so did his sister Sofia. So family would always be dropping in—and so did their many friends. "In a way, they all helped raise Gia," says Jacqui. "We had parties 'cause we didn't want babysitters," she explains. "So Gia became everyone's little angel. [Famed video director] Mark Romanek was like an uncle to her. There'd be parties going on here, and he'd be watching three hours of *Little Mermaid* with her in the den. It was like a village taking care of her. Of course, these days, she's actually hanging out with friends of mine, like Liz [a filmmaker, jewelry designer, and a scion of the famed Goldwyn family of old Hollywood]. They're going to a movie together tonight."

The form of group nurturing led to more and better parties at what became the Coppola/Getty home, after Jacqui met and married Peter Getty. Particularly, it led to the evolution of Jacqui's famed annual Halloween parties, which are now legendary and have featured such highlights as Steven Cojocaru dressed as Donatella Versace (and nearly stumping the real Naomi Campbell), Sofia Coppola dressed as Yoko Ono, writer/producer Mitch Glazer doing a fabulous Robert Evans take-off, and *Vogue* West Coast editor Lisa Love teaming up with actress Kelly Lynch to portray Siegfried and Roy—not without large stuffed cats.

"The Halloween parties started two years before Gia stopped trick or treating," Jacqui recalls. "Because we wanted to hang out with her. So we'd trick or treat, then come home and get the party started. Uncle Francis usually comes. One year he came as an Indian chief, one year he came with a hula skirt on. And one year he just got mad and sat in the corner with a suit on."

With dressing in costume a prerequisite, and truckloads of "scary" furniture moving in and out during Halloween week, the party's reached a fever pitch of hot ticket–ness to Hollywood flamboyants. "The party goes to six a.m. and the house is destroyed," Jacqui sighs. "I liked when I did all the cooking myself, and I used my own silver. Now it's gone to another level of valets and caterers. Bryan Rabin [a well-established L.A. party planner] has to help me out. One year I had Krispy Kreme show up with doughnuts—and everyone thought that was the greatest costume."

No doubt, it's wise for her to avoid risking her own well-honed furniture, which, while lived in and comfortable, still has history and pedigree. Her dining room hosts a 1940s Blackman Cruz dining-room table that came from a monastery library in Italy. Its vintage chairs, a gift from friend Bridget Romanek, have red leather doughnut-shape backs—but as there were too few of them, "we had some made." The nearby sideboard, made from 1930s wood and copper, holds Jacqui's prized china and silver collection: Tiffany Audubon silver, crystal glasses, tea sets from Tiffany's, and Puiforcat silver.

A white leather Billy Haines chair sits nearby, surrounded by a Lucite table, a Chinese cabinet from one of Jacqui's favorite stores, J. F. Chen, and many collectibles from family trips (with both the Gettys and the Coppolas) to Turkey, Morocco, China, and Tuscany. The den is practically covered with family photographs, many of them shot by Jacqui's pal, famed photographer Paul Jasmine. Lush exotic backyard areas are packed with Moroccan pillows, tables, and lamps—enough to make Talitha Getty proud. If these Moroccan tables could talk . . .

They might tell stories about the night Mick Jagger dropped by for one of Jacqui's parties, then casually happened to mention that a tow truck was towing somebody's car. Or the night the Smashing Pumpkins wreaked havoc. Or how a sushi chef cut fresh sushi in the living room at a party for director Wes Anderson. Or how Jacqui herself cooked a recent dinner for Demi Moore and Ashton Kutcher, Anjelica Huston and Robert Graham, Chloë Sevigny, Selma Blair, Johnson Hartig of Libertine, the stylist Arianne Phillips—and how everybody always hangs out in the kitchen when she's cooking. "There could be the most wonderful photography book of my parties," she sighs. "I remember a night we all sat on the roof drinking wine. When I woke up, there were still a lot of people here—so what did I do? I cooked breakfast." But the parties are among Hollywood's most protected secrets, and unlike many other festivities, are still for insiders only.

Another part of the house with its share of stories is her newly converted bedroom closet, fit, as it is, for a fashion archivist. "It used to be the nanny's room," she says. "Now it's all heavy, heavy beautiful wood." That, with a lot of Marc Jacobs, Lanvin, Chloe, Zac Posen, Rick Owens, and of course, a couple of Chanel couture dresses. "The first time I went to the Paris couture shows, Ann, Peter's mother, decided that the husband's family should buy the bride a trousseau. Her idea of that was three Chanel couture dresses. Well, as a stylist, I'd been hanging out with models. I went to meet her at Chanel in Paris wearing a down jacket and Ugg boots and a ponytail. The women who worked there took one look at me, and said, 'Madame, *you* do not have an appointment.' Finally, I said, 'I'm with Mrs. Getty,' and they let me in—but they thought I was her assistant!"

While she's been known to lend clothes to girlfriends and her daughter, Jacqui herself—unlike most well-known social stylish L.A. ladies—never borrows clothes. Never. She is the Oprah Winfrey of the L.A. fashion set. "I buy everything," she says. "I'm a big buyer. I love clothes, and I want to support the designers I support. Now I've turned my mother-in-law on to some other ways of dressing: before me, she only bought couture. Now she wears Alber, Rick Owens, Marc Jacobs, and even Juicy during the day. I introduced her to prêt-à-porter, and I'm really proud of that. She loves it."

Jacqui's newer style obsessions include the Jean Paul Gaultier–designed Birkin bag and vintage jewelry: a vintage Bulgari watch and 1950s, '60s, and '70s diamond and gold pieces. "Ann gave me a few pieces like that, and I became obsessed. She's my foremost style inspiration."

Meanwhile, with all this style floating around the house, it still has a hippie rustic quality that comes from the neighborhood it's in, and as much as Jacqui—and her husband, Peter, who favors Rat Pack era suits—love clothes, many of their pals are jeans and T-shirt devotees. And that's just fine. It's come as you are—or—come as you wish you could be. Anything goes. "Everything about this house," she smiles, "is pure from its heart. There's no pretention. It's a safe haven. That's why everybody comes here."

A white leather chair by actor-turned-furniture-designer/decorator Billy Haines sits in the corner of the charming dining room, next to a 1930s wood and copper sideboard, with one-of-a-kind Italian marble pieces from Blackman Cruz resting on top.

The red Chinese cabinet with decorative gold inlay came from a little antiques store on Melrose Avenue called J. F. Chen. Two paintings ("fake Modiglianis—we have them because I covet an original!" says Jacqui) sit on the mantel above the original fireplace.

Photos of Jacqui's two extended families—the Coppolas and the Gettys—fill the casual TV room. Small accents, like an Hermès blanket thrown over the arm of a Ligne Roset couch covered in canvas and colorful Navajo pillows, give the house a relaxed and informal feel.

If these walls could talk: many well-known musicians have played a song or two on the baby grand piano (tucked away behind the yellow chair) during one of Peter and Jacqui's famous Halloween parties, which generally last into the wee hours.

"Everything about this house is pure from the heart. It's a safe haven."

Jacqui and Peter favor animal prints and stay warm with the lush fur blanket and throw pillows on the bed. A black and white photograph, which was a gift from good friend Demi Moore, sits on a bookcase that contains their collection of valuable first-edition art and photography books. Mirrored lamps top side tables that "I will keep forever," says Jacqui. "They are very sentimental—a gift from my friend Steven, who has since passed away."

Previously the nanny's room, Jacqui's stunning dark wood custom-made closet houses her enormous collection of Hermès Birkin bags, Alaia shoes, Lanvin dresses (by good friend Alber Elbaz) and dozens of caftans. She says, "I do have a lot of caftans . . . I don't go out at night in them; I wear them at home—I'm a real home-girl, you know."

Jacqui's daughter, Gia, graduated from high school last fall and recently completed an internship at French *Vogue*. Her bedroom door is adorned with telltale signs of a teenager: stickers for rock bands, movies, and clothing lines (like Milk Fed, whose designer is cousin Sofia Coppola). The great American photographer Joseph Szabo gave the black and white photograph at right to Gia.

Jacqui has created her own Moroccan den on the back patio, with pillows she brought back from Turkey and one-of-a-kind pieces found on a trip to China with Ann and Gordon Getty. The oversized wicker swivel chair from California Living with green and gold striped cushion is a much coveted and collected item.

Jacqui, in a tan Lanvin dress, relaxes in her outdoor living room. A legendary entertainer, Getty routinely throws parties where guests such as Mick Jagger, Robert Evans, and the Smashing Pumpkins often stop by.

Stylish. Modern. Fabulous. These words describe *Sex and the City*'s Carrie Bradshaw and could just as easily fit the house that the show's creator and executive producer, Darren Star, lives in. But like Carrie, there is much more to this chic ultra-modern house than meets the eye. "To execute something that looks deceptively simple is sometimes really hard and is very interesting to me," says Star. Much as he has done with the popular series he has created over the past decade (*Beverly Hills 90210, Melrose Place,* and the aforementioned *Sex and the City*), Star has created a living space that is hard to forget once you experience it. With the help of architect Mark Rios of Rios Clementi Hale Studios, Star set about turning the house, designed in the 1950s by Hal Levitt, into an interesting multidimensional environment that hooks you the minute you walk up to it. The front entry of smooth concrete and frosted glass accented by concrete pavers and ironwood planks offers an entrance as sexy and theatrical as any of his shows.

Since growing up in a very modern house, Star has always been drawn to contemporary architecture. He loves the work of the legendary modernist master Brazilian architect Oscar Niemeyer. Known for the dynamic sensual curves and "pavilion" feeling of his spaces, Niemeyer worked with Le Corbusier and Wallace Harrison on the United Nations headquarters in New York. Star wanted to incorporate both of these aspects of Niemeyer's work into his home. He is also a Richard Neutra fan, and lived in a house designed by the late famed L.A. modern architect Charles Kanner in Malibu prior to this residence. "Los Angeles is a city that is home to a lot of great modern architecture, but I wanted to do it in a comfortable way. Doing this house was a way to kind of explore that."

To achieve this thoroughly modern—and very L.A.—aesthetic, Star and architect Mark Rios worked closely to open up the house by not only adding eight hundred square feet but also creating deliberate "constant connections with the outdoors." They had the landscaping completely redone to create a "wet outdoor living room," with a fourteen-by-thirty-five-foot swimming pool in the center. A submerged bench runs the spacious length of the pool, creating a unique space for Star and friends to enjoy a cosmopolitan or two. The back corner of the pool features a raised spa with two waterfalls, one spilling smoothly back into the pool and the other flowing into a sunken rock garden. On one side of the pool a long, rectangular ironwood deck holds sleek lounge chairs and planters of colorful native flora. Supported by thirteen caissons driven into the bedrock hillside, the deck extends the small yard by twelve feet. Star had the hedges torn down to extend the views from all sides. A bed of resilient, newly planted dichondra grass forms an ultra cool "outside" carpet between the house and the swimming pool.

With its large glass walls, doors, and windows, the house offers the feeling of being inside and outside at the same time. "There are a lot of examples of these types of houses around the country; Philip Johnson's Glass House is probably the most well known, but [indoor/outdoor living] particularly works well in Los Angeles because of the weather. You are really able to have the experience all year round." Natural material elements that are used both indoors and outdoors also blur the boundaries and add to the sense of flow. Star has spent quite a bit of time in Indonesia and loves the fresh and modern feeling of the indigenous homes, especially in Bali. "They all have a lot of natural woods," he notes, and he wanted to incorporate a little bit of that feeling into the house. Star also had bamboo planted around the property's perimeter not only to maintain privacy but also to give the house a bit of that Eastern flavor. The all-ironwood decks extend into the addition in one place bringing the natural materials-elements directly inside.

Star has been an avid modern art collector for a number of years, but with no great places in his former homes to hang the art. When thinking about the renovation of this new house, deciding where the art—including a number of works he owns by Ed Ruscha—should go in the space was the most fun for him. Star worked with interior designer Milo Baglioni to incorporate the art into the decor. "The house is very much about the art," he asserts. It was important that the balance of shapes and colors or the feeling or mood of the art could be seen or experienced from the best vantage point possible but also that the decor provided a clean, uncluttered, and comfortable environment in which to view it. Baglioni used contemporary furnishings in soft upholstery and neutral colors to create the desired effect.

Star looks for the same qualities in interior design that he looks for in his art: specific and designed—but not overtly so—stylish, comfortable, and clean. Not very interested in narrative art, Star has much more of a minimalist sensibility: "I can appreciate a white painting." One of the reasons he is such a fan of Ruscha's is because at first glance, "the work seems very simple but as you look closely at the detail of brushstrokes and the variations of color, you see things that are not as simple as you thought." The physical interior of the house has very clean lines with no visible moldings. A lack of ornate decoration leaves the walls exposed in a way that allows one to notice the imperfections. "It is in the complication where you can hide imperfections. It's so much harder to make something simple than it is to make something complicated," says Star.

Though the house predictably has immense style, it has a lot of warmth in keeping with Star's wish that the house "feel like a home and not like a magazine layout." He thinks of it as a very comfortable, happy house. This "smart house" has great electronics built in and is exceptionally wired for music and television. Star installed a hidden projector in the living room; it was "the first thing I did in the house and it is my very favorite toy," he says. He loves watching movies there and lying on the couch in the glass walled addition, feeling surrounded by nature.

Like the rest of the residence, the new pool room addition is almost seamlessly connected to the landscape. The ironwood from the outdoor deck reaches into the room, where it meets flush with the white terrazzo floor. Floor-to-ceiling steel and glass doors slide on tracks that extend beyond the house so the room can be opened to the outdoors. Star thought the space originally intended to be his workspace was too spectacular to use as "my big messy office." He admits that his office at home (he also has one on the Sony lot) has a much different feeling than the rest of the house. It may be one of the very few places that the clean and clutter-free aspect of his modern aesthetic goes astray. The space is darker than the rest of the house and scripts pile up on his desk. Above all of the clutter and organized chaos, however, hangs a painting of a simple question mark by Ed Ruscha, perhaps reminding Star that the disorder comes and goes, no matter how much you try to keep it at bay. Wherever there's an intentionally ordered, clean surface—minimalist at its finest—something big and creative is lurking nearby.

Previous page: Star has owned several architecturally important homes in Los Angeles, including a Charles Kanner–designed Malibu retreat. He completed renovation of his current home in 2001.

The long drive up to the house is "an important part of the entry sequence," according to architect Mark Rios. His firm created the new driveway with sandblasted, slate-colored concrete and refinished the exterior of the house in smooth-troweled plaster.

Rios focused on the importance of the front windows and entry: "We designed it in a kind of hide and reveal style, focusing on the Ed Ruscha painting of the stars (visible in the photograph on page 29)." Guests walk on the raised deck, passing by the glass-enclosed guest room and office, which have gaps on the side, to give little slices of a view. A ginkgo grove is planted inside and outside of the courtyard.

Rios Clementi Hale Studios chose a clean, modern aesthetic to reflect both the existing house and the sophisticated lifestyle of Star. The architects wanted to open up spaces as much as possible, creating constant connections with the outdoors. Large glass walls, doors, and windows (some of them pivoting) contribute to dematerializing the boundaries between inside and out.

In the modern den two Calder crème leather and chrome sofas by Minotti are paired with a custom-designed white lacquered oak coffee table. The curvy little peanut-shaped side table was made by Robert Kuo Designs, in hand-hammered bronze. Greeting visitors as they enter the home is *Paint Chip Painting* by Peter Wegner (visible near the door at left). *Big Dipper* by Ed Ruscha hangs on the wall at right.

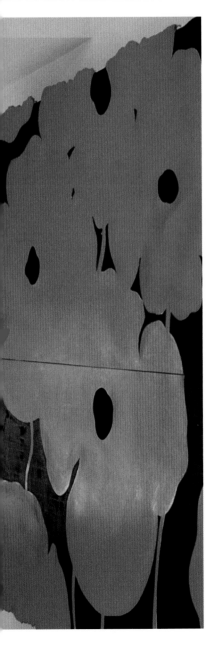

It is difficult to decide what the most impressive element in the home office is—the Ed Ruscha painting, the Golden Globes, or the Emmy Award. A photograph on one of the bronze shelves in the rift-sawn oak cabinet of striking *Sex and the City* star and friend Sarah Jessica Parker stands out, next to a custom-designed hand-waxed leather sofa.

The guest bathroom, with its distinctive custom-designed mosaic mirror, reflects interior designer Milo Baglioni's attention to detail throughout the home. He found the Thor light fixtures at DIVA in Los Angeles and paired them with a Philippe Starck faucet and stainless-steel and wood sink.

Only the creator of *Beverly Hills 90210, Melrose Place,* and *Sex and the City* could get away with an opulent faux ostrich leather and mahogany custom-made bed. The bed is framed by a pair of *panneaux de verre* mahogany side tables, embellished with hand-painted glass panels and bronze bamboo motif. A retro Delaunay cord-colored leather and chrome chair is by Minotti, behind which hangs a piece by renowned Cuban artist Enrique Celaya.

Star's collection of illustrated books focuses on art and artist-made volumes and is displayed in a custom-made walnut and bronze cabinet by Ian Walmsley Design. The blue doors are by L.A. sculptor Robert Therrien.

The elegant pool room has floor-to-ceiling steel and glass doors that slide on tracks that extend beyond the house for "inside living outdoors." Walnut chairs accompany a Chambord limestone table, all by Christian Liaigre for Holly Hunt.

"It is in the complication where you can hide imperfections. It's so much harder to make something simple than it is to make something complicated."

A "wet outdoor living room" was created in the backyard, centered on a fourteen-by-thirty-five-foot swimming pool. The back corner of the pool is a raised spa with two waterfalls, one spilling smoothly back into the pool and the other flowing into a sunken rock garden. The river rock trough at right appears to flow from the exterior through the living room of the house and out the other side.

Glamour. If you are not one of the very few lucky ones born with it, chances are you look for it somewhere else—in movies, television, magazines, or books. If you follow the path of writer/director Ryan Murphy, creator of the fabulously subversive hit television show *nip/tuck,* you find it every day in your very own house. Carl Maston, a professor of architecture at the University of Southern California in the 1960s (with other renowned faculty members Craig Ellwood and Ralph Knowles), built the residence for his family in 1948. The house "feels very organic with its redwood walls and has a great New Regency glamour to it," says Murphy. The moment he walked in, Murphy knew it was the house for him. He rented the house for a year, finally purchasing it in April of 2001.

The previous owner of the home had just completed a four-year architectural refurbishment, so Murphy has spent most of his time and energy on its interior decor. Taking cues from the house's inherent glamour while adding the signature sense of modernism that informs all of his creative work, Murphy hired interior designer Diane Rosenstein to help him achieve his goal of making the house "a cross between a Big Sur house and a George Cukor movie." Though Murphy wanted to be a purist about everything, using authentic pieces from or reproduced to match the period that the house was built (1946–48), he wanted glamour without slickness. To that end, he has also used a number of touches from the late 1970s—his favorite example being a painting he found at auction of actress Candice Bergen in China that was commissioned for a *Playboy* magazine cover. The much-loved piece hangs in his bedroom. For Murphy, the late 1940s and the late '70s are almost identical in their aesthetic, so he liked the idea of "smashing them up" against each other.

Films from the 1970s, "a time when I was coming of age and forming my aesthetic," Murphy offers, also greatly inspired his choices for the decor. Roman Polanski's *Rosemary's Baby* is his favorite film and he admits that there are definite touches of it visible in the house. Murphy is also a tremendous fan of production designer Ferdinando Scarfiotti, who worked on two of Italian director Bernardo Bertolucci's most famous films, *Last Tango in Paris* and *The Conformist*. Scarfiotti also worked on Paul Schrader's *American Gigolo,* a film Murphy feels could have been shot in his house, as "it really is an adult boy house, the ultimate bachelor pad." Designed with a lot of water elements, it is also "a very sensual house," Murphy adds.

The house is arranged in a clean, simple, and organized way, with the specific purpose of relating to the pristine lines of the original design. "It is a very modern structure that gives you the feeling that you can't make a mess . . . that if something were out of place you'd have to demolish it!" says Murphy.

The house itself is like a piece of organic art. The tremendous amount of bare wooden wall space seems to create a dialogue with visitors. Much thought went into choosing furniture to fit in with the structure of the house and with the overall aesthetic Ryan was looking to achieve. There are pieces by Jean-Michel Frank and Jean Prouve in the house as well as a lot by British-born T. H. Robsjohn-Gibbings and other midcentury designers. "I like the period of design from 1945 to 1950 before it got very kitschy," Murphy says. "It is very European and is a new age sort of period in American culture and I am very inspired by it." There is also a rare Paava Tynell Snowflake chandelier above his dining table, which he wanted his whole life and finally found at an estate auction.

Murphy's home is very much like a movie set or a sound stage. There is a sense of serenity and quiet that almost seems unnatural but also an organic buzz that makes the house feel like a living, breathing thing. "There is a hum to the house that energizes me when I wake up in the morning and when I go to bed at night," he says. Murphy augmented the calm presence of nature outside by adding a Japanese maple garden and a Japanese soaking tub. The versatility of the indoor and outdoor living spaces also creates a feeling of simultaneous calm and activity that really attracted Murphy to the house. After growing up in the Midwest, where "in September the windows went down and were not open again until April," Murphy treasures the fact that every window and every door in the house is designed to swing open to bring the air and the elements inside.

Much like the relationship between Drs. Troy and McNamara on *nip/tuck,* Murphy's living and working environments evoke a seemingly uniform feeling, but upon closer examination there are many distinct layers beneath the surface. Though his work tends to come across as very dark and cynical, it more often than not contains deep and complicated emotion. Murphy is very interested in the notion of slamming together two sensibilities that one would think are complete opposites but are actually very similar. Murphy says that as a director "the biggest thing you can do,

I think, is to know what the tone of something is." In putting together the interior decor of the house, he very much wanted visitors to the house to feel its tone the minute they walk in. The home embodies his dream aesthetic of organic meets Hollywood glamour and he feels in some ways that it is the epitome of both sides of his personality. This dichotomy is reflected in two of his favorite pieces of furniture in the house—a pair of cabinets that Diane Rosenstein helped him design. Murphy had them painted very specific colors—one to match the color of the swimming pool in the day and the other to match the color of the pool at night. The pieces really embody the themes of complementary opposites—light and dark, inside and outside, natural and unnatural light—that Murphy loves so much. Murphy will also go through phases where he becomes obsessed with certain colors and he will redo the sets on the show and his house with them. His office on the lot is decorated and designed almost exactly like his home. Modernism and minimalism inform his life and his work constantly.

As an artist whose head is so chaotically filled with stories, Murphy wanted to create a home where "the space is relaxed and forces you to be so." He also wanted the house to be a place where you can recover from the onslaught of your life, where you can recharge and energize yourself to get the strength to go back into the world again. In addition, it was important to him to create a place "where people in your life can also feel like it is their home in some weird way." Judging from the number of people who frequently drop by to swim or use the soaking tub, he seems to have gotten his wish.

With a house that embodies glamour with a hint of mystery, a hit television show that does the same, and feature films under his belt with the likes of Annette Bening, Meryl Streep, and Gwyneth Paltrow, the question "What don't you like about yourself?" is a pretty difficult one for Ryan Murphy to answer.

Previous page: Cantilevered windows line the pool and, when opened on a cool L.A. evening with the fire going, create the ideal indoor/outdoor living and dining room. A teal Billy Haines cabinet adds a dash of color in the corner.

Originally a journalist, Murphy eventually got into screenwriting and penned the pilot for *nip/tuck*.
In the master bedroom, an Irving Penn photograph of Faye Dunaway hangs behind Ryan—just
one picture from his extensive photography collection.

It's hard to imagine Murphy writing his psychologically intense hit show in the calm and serene home office. Beautiful photogravures from Karl Blossfeldt's "Urformen der Kunst" (1928) series line the wall above a T. H. Robsjohn-Gibbings 1950s green settee. The Greta Grossman coffee table complements the Chinese Jesus custom walnut desk perfectly.

Builder Ken Duran of Duran+Associates worked to maintain the natural elements of the home, seen in the custom colored concrete floors and the refurbished brick fireplace.

Carl Maston, who taught at USC in the 1960s with other illustrious architects of the time like Craig Ellwood, originally built the home for himself. Interior designers Rosenstein and Witke selected pieces that reflect the great midcentury design, like the green Harvey Probber cabinet in the first-floor hallway. The vintage French light fixtures are from the 1950s.

The home embodies Murphy's dream aesthetic of organic meets Hollywood glamour. . . . It is the epitome of both sides of his personality.

The vintage yellow dining chairs in the kitchen create a soft contrast with the clean lines and purity of the structure. A stunning table of Lucite and walnut custom-made by Chinese Jesus is illuminated by a Hans Wegner pendant light. *Nude* (1989), a photograph by Glen Elder, hangs on the wall, and just beyond, a custom steel staircase with cork treads leads to the second floor.

The original wood ceiling is painted white, and the rich plank walls made of redwood were refinished. All of the perfect period furniture is centered on an Edward Fields gold, white, and tan print area rug from the 1960s. A 1950s Harvey Probber glass-topped coffee table is surrounded by a flawless pair of white Edward Wormley sofas. Paul McCobb white ottomans and a set of wrought-iron chairs with white cushions designed by Billy Haines balance the other side. On a console behind the couch sits a brass tripod table lamp by T. H. Robsjohn-Gibbings.

A luminous and quite rare brass handmade fixture by Finnish artist Paavo Tynell, circa 1950, hangs over the walnut dining table by Baker Furniture from the 1960s. A custom built-in sideboard almost disappears into the redwood walls under the delirious Scott Lifshutz painting, *Miss Universe* (1999).

Murphy recently made his feature film directorial debut with the adaptation of Augusten Burroughs's novel *Running with Scissors*, starring Annette Bening, Gwyneth Paltrow, and Joseph Fiennes.

The master bedroom is distinctly midcentury minimal, but the interior design "adds a bit of elegance and luxury, reflecting Ryan's personality," offers interior designer Rosenstein. Architect Steven Slan designed the sleek steel fireplace and concrete hearth that anchors the room. A vintage Edward Fields hand-woven wool area rug from the 1960s rests on the cork tile floor. The custom-made bed is flanked by night tables from Baker Furniture, circa 1960.

High in the Hollywood Hills, Murphy's property boasts staggering views, while retaining utter seclusion behind the protection of exotic trees, hedges, and landscaping. Stairs lead from the terrace off of the master bedroom down to a forty-foot lap pool.

Demme's magnetic personality and cool sensibility have made her bars at the Roosevelt Hotel the hottest places to be almost every night of the week. The only problem is the precious little time that leaves for relaxing at home.

Amanda Scheer Demme is a truly modern Renaissance woman—of and undoubtedly ahead of her time. A veritable force to be reckoned with, she has helped to define how and where hip modern culture socializes, whom they listen to, and what they will be doing next. As a multifaceted business-woman, Demme just "knows what's up." It is that instinct that has made her an unbelievably successful music supervisor for films (*Mean Girls, Garden State, Out of Sight, Blow*), artist man-ager (Cypress Hill, House of Pain, Nikka Costa, Mark Ronson), label owner (with bands such as Korn and Incubus), event pro-moter, and entrepreneur. There is seemingly no end to the knowl-edge, energy, and enthusiasm that she puts into each of these fields of "lifestyle production"; she has come not only to master them but also to leave her indelible mark upon them.

Demme says, "One of the great ironies of my life is that I went to culinary school," but she has been moving toward where she is today since high school, when she worked as a production assis-tant at a radio station after classes. Demme worked the door at seminal New York City club the World, where she heard bands like Jane's Addiction for the first time. She did stints at hotels like the Four Seasons and the Morgan (the last hotel owned by the infamous Steve Rubell) and ran her own weekly hip-hop underground club that brought the legendary Kid Capri from the Bronx to the downtown set for the very first time. Even if she didn't know it then, Demme has always been and continues to be a trailblazer and trendsetter—mixing up themes, scenes, and people to create environments that both inform and interest her. Always trying to be "forward thinking," she finds huge inspiration in everything and everyone around her.

A natural observer and "student of culture," Demme would rather be among "people who are much more visionary than I am," listening to what they know, than be the center of attention. Friends like photographer and publisher Lisa Eisner greatly inspire her. "Lisa just knows art so well. I try to surround myself with people that are really smart about what they do and I really enjoy listening to them," Demme says. Her passions include looking at old books and vintage couture clothes, watching classic movies (*All About Eve, Chinatown, The Graduate*), and listening to music. Some of her greatest inspiration comes from going out at night and experiencing different scenes. "I love to watch the kids that are the trendsetters; seeing what they are into or not into and adapting it to a more mainstream mentality," she says.

Demme and her two children (Jaxson and Dexter) have lived in three different houses in just as many years. Her ability to adapt long term to her environment was tragically hindered by the sudden death of her husband, director Ted Demme (*Blow, Beautiful Girls*) on January 13, 2001. "After Teddy's death, nothing felt like home." Each house, with the exception of the first one, she completely gutted and remade from scratch. Though Demme loved her previous case-study-like house—"a house in the sky"—it had no yard for her kids. So in looking for her next home, outdoor space was put high on the list of requirements.

Their current residence was more than she could have asked for: an ultramodern house with a large yard set up against the Santa Monica Conservatory, which offers incredible privacy and is five minutes from her kids' school. Starting with her now trademark MO to gut and completely remodel, Demme designed the house floor to ceiling herself without using a contractor or architect. It helped that she had just done a house less than eighteen months prior. Armed with her Rolodex of subcontractors—plumbers, wall guys, electricians, floor guys—Demme knew exactly what she wanted and who would get it done quickly and correctly. With a nod to her love for modern designers Demme worked to create a seamless indoor/outdoor space with windows and floors that give you the impression that the inside floats into and out of the outside.

In her efficient, self-assured way, Demme demonstrated an amazing sense of adaptability to get the renovation done in her own time. Though she admits to "designing based on availability" and buying items "off the floor" because of her distaste for waiting months for things to arrive from Italy, her design style by no means implies that things that are "available" don't fit masterfully in the spaces she deems for them. The Italian doors for her kitchen slide in a particular way that she loves, but the hardware cannot be found in the United States. So Demme had her own versions made to avoid the wait, and they work perfectly. If an item she likes was not "made for her space," she redesigns the space based on what's there and makes the item work. Sometimes this means putting things together that were not made to be together, but she knows that this comes with the territory.

Demme says that before her husband passed away, her taste ran more toward the Gothic and exotic—"dark, heavy, and ominous"—as well as Chinese and Moroccan design. Knickknacks abounded and the "stuff" piled up. Since his death, her aesthetic

has changed considerably; it is almost completely about clean lines and surfaces now. She wants no clutter or unnecessary excess in her life at all. A great woman of style who cites JaneMary (a local designer sold exclusively at Maxfield's), Balenciaga, and Rick Owens as her design inspirations, she gives away clothes that she doesn't foresee wearing anymore. This clutter-free lifestyle, she says, has given "such order to my life."

This same pared down aesthetic is also directly reflected in the pieces that she has chosen for her home. Each piece with its clean lines and lack of excess is both eclectic and chic. Demme loves mixing old and new—beautiful vintage 1960s and early 1970s furniture from all over the world with modern pieces like her B&B Italian leather sofa. The kitchen cabinets are thoroughly modern, made out of lacquer and frosted glass, so even though they are used daily, they always look "super fresh." As she constantly rearranges and changes the furniture, Demme sees the house, much like her work, as her painting palette.

Her talent and taste carry over into her public life, too. Brought in as an owner, face, and lifestyle producer for the bars at the historic Roosevelt Hotel in Hollywood, the Tropicana Lobby Bar, and the aptly named Teddy's, her job was to motivate the hotel's designer to try to achieve her needs. Inspired by renowned California architect John Lautner (Demme is a self-confessed "freak" for his work) the Lautner Palm Springs vibe of her bar and cabanas turned out beautifully and has attracted the likes of every hot young celebrity (think Lindsay Lohan), tastemaker (stylist Rachel Zoe), and entertainment power player (think Ted Field) out there. You name them and they have been a guest of Amanda's.

Although she has been an advocate for preservation and restoration, Demme found the constraints of working on a historical building difficult. However, the experience has taught her a tremendous amount; she learned that she really loves owning a bar and now knows how different the design and maintenance of hotel spaces is from one's own house.

With that said, Demme sees her future in designing her own bars and hotels . . . maybe starting with a bar within a hotel and then moving on to designing a boutique hotel. With a talent for always being ahead of her time, combining the eclectic with the specific and mixing the old with a new, one can only expect that Amanda Scheer Demme's next venture will entertain, inform, and excite us all.

Demme did not work with a decorator but instead chose to design the interior herself, searching the world for each piece in the home with the help of her friend Cliff Wong. In the dining room is a Danish teak and brass table by Hans Wegner, paired with chairs by Michel Cadestin, originally produced for the Centre Pompidou in Paris. Against the wall is a 1952 Paul McCobb wall unit with vintage Raymor bookends by Ben Seibel, circa 1950.

The entertainment room feels a bit retro, with a shag rug and a 1950s color scheme—a fun surprise from the ultrahip nightlife queen of Los Angeles. Vintage Danish leather Swan chairs stand out, as does an elegant cocktail table from Herman Miller. A funky metal shelving unit adorns the wall.

Demme enclosed the property in a substantial poured-concrete fence that separates her home from an adjacent preserve, providing a tremendous amount of privacy. Glass doors open off the living room and lead out to a patio filled with comfortable lounge furniture from California Living.

Leather floor cushions provide casual seating by the contemporary concrete fireplace at the center of the room, lined with German ceramics. The vintage linen and canvas Pernilla chair by Bruno Mathsson was imported from the Netherlands.

The ultraclean kitchen features stainless-steel Italian appliances, chocolate lacquered and frosted glass cabinets, and a cool terrazzo floor. "I just wanted absolutely no clutter," says Demme, "very modern, very Jetsons . . . a kitchen where it looks like the food almost cooks itself!"

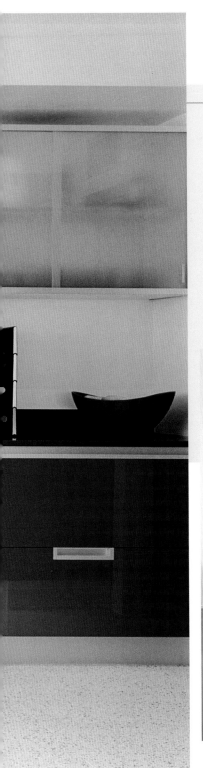

"I just wanted absolutely no clutter . . . very modern, very Jetsons . . . a kitchen where it looks like the food almost cooks itself!"

Important vintage pieces fill Demme's home. A classic leather lounge chair and ottoman by Brazilian Sergio Rodrigues sit next to a red vintage cocktail table. A handmade black walnut floor lamp by Michael Wilson is visible in the background.

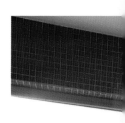

A dramatic and contemporary double-height chrome and frosted glass closet in the master bedroom houses Demme's collection of Rick Owens T-shirts, Balenciaga, Christian Dior Homme jackets, and dozens of pairs of True Religion, Mogg, and vintage Levi's jeans. A 1966 string and leather Jorgen Hovelskov lounge chair is accentuated with a red throw. Sliding doors at right lead to yet another closet, dressing area, and the master bath.

Demme's extensive and eclectic mix of everything from stilettos to Converse high-tops rivals that of Carrie Bradshaw. The meticulously kept shoe closet was custom designed to hold over one hundred pairs of shoes as well as her very cool hat collection.

Bright red tile gleams in the modern guest bath—quite a departure from the dark and ominous Gothic look that Demme's former homes were known for.

Demme's background is in music—she owned a boutique record label with acts like D'Angelo, Nikki Costa, and Mark Ronson, and she is the creator of sound tracks for films like *Garden State* and *Blow*.

The story goes that when a certain young, tall, Alabama-bred blonde walked into the Monkey Bar in Hollywood in 1992, Steve Tisch took one look, turned to his guy friends, and said: "Uh-oh. I think I'm going to marry that girl."

Three years later he did, and he and Jamie Tisch now have five-year-old twins and a seven-year-old (in addition to twenty-one- and seventeen-year-old kids from his first marriage). "Steve's still telling that story about the night we met," she laughs. "But he never said that to me. He's always very sure of what he wants. And I can barely decide what to have for lunch! But there's a lot that is fortuitous in our relationship. For instance, Steve came to the house we now own when he was fifteen, to go to a party with his parents that former owners Freddie Fields and Polly Bergen were throwing!" Little did he know he and his expanded family would reside there years later.

"We looked at a number of houses," says Jamie. "And I wasn't all that familiar with the L.A. architects of the thirties and forties, like Paul Williams. I knew the feeling I wanted—a little Georgian—and when we walked in, I just loved this house right away. It's got the perfect scale—not enormous—and the fact that it's on a cul-de-sac makes it very private. And the amount of acreage it's on makes it very special, even for Los Angeles." Williams, who designed the Tisches' home, created homes and buildings for fifty years, leaving a legacy that helps define the visual landscape of chic contemporary Los Angeles. He reworked the landmark Beverly Hills Hotel in the late 1940s and is the person responsible for all of that recognizable pink and green.

Even with their outstanding art collection, French antique furniture, and a chandelier from Gianni Versace's Milan apartment, the house is somehow still comfortable enough for the three little kids and two chocolate labs, all of whom bound about with an abandon you wouldn't expect in this environment. "The house is not that fancy," Jamie claims. "It's sort of indestructible. Except for the artwork. And I don't remember having to tell the kids, 'Get your hands off that painting'—well, okay, maybe once!"

Jamie's influence can be seen and felt all around the house, which she's constantly updating with small—or large—touches. "I redecorated Steve's office recently. It was this dark mahogany color with faux finishes over it for years—even sanded down, it wasn't that smooth. I wanted to infuse some color into the house, so we painted the walls in the office sage green. This made it less dark. And I rearranged some of the artwork in there." Along with the art, the crown jewel is the Oscar Steve won for producing Best Picture of 1994, *Forrest Gump.*

Jamie and Steve handpicked the art collection, which includes works by Ed Ruscha, Howard Hodgkin, Francesco Clemente, and Georgia O'Keeffe. "We've never worked with a curator to find our art," Jamie explains. "It tends to be landscapes, which is what we love. It varies wildly. We never buy a piece for a certain spot in the house, and we move them around a lot. You get a fresh perspective when you change something around. I just put a new Ruscha in the dining room. We don't have huge pieces of art for the most part, so it's easy to do."

The Tisches are well known for holding charity events at their home—which often include outdoor fetes on the tennis court and front entrance lawn—but are even better known for their near-weekly screenings. When at home in Los Angeles, neighbors and friends like photographer Danica Perez and her husband Charles; Lisa Kudrow and her husband, Michel Stern; and next-door neighbors Janet and Gunnar Peterson (the trainer to the stars who helped Steve Tisch when he famously lost a hundred pounds in the last few years) come over for what Jamie describes as a dinner of "clean food—unless I'm going Southern, and then it's fried!" and a screening of a first-run movie that probably hasn't even opened yet. This is how insiders in the movie business entertain at home.

But there have also been large fetes produced by party planner extraordinaire Ben Bourjois, a friend of Jamie's, for the charity nearest to her heart, the Women's Cancer Research Fund, formerly associated with Cedars Sinai Hospital in Beverly Hills but now a more national effort. Hosting guests at the WCRF event, like Angela Janklow, designer Tory Burch (in from New York), Lisa and Eric Eisner, Jim and Elizabeth Wiatt, the Tisches' landscape architect (and hairdresser!) Art Luna, and decorator Tim Clark, Jamie wore a knockout Oscar de la Renta tiered-pouf dress with beading, proving that her frequent New York visits are having a big effect on her fashion sense.

Always one of Los Angeles' best dressed, and a former national sales director for a clothing company, Jamie and the family uprooted in 2005 and spent a year living in the Regency Hotel in Manhattan, where Steve could be closer to his family. (The hotel falls under the umbrella of the Loews Corporation, which the Tisch

family owns.) For a girl raised in Alabama who's lived in Los Angeles most of her adult life, it was a big transition. "I was intimidated by New York before I lived there," she admits. "But people there were so much nicer than I expected them to be. And living in close proximity always has people offering to come pick you up. At first, I was taking my kids to school in dresses and heels. Now I'm more relaxed there—and I realize I can take them to school in jeans. But *not* pajamas or sweatpants, like I do in L.A.!"

Jamie's fashion journey began in her native Alabama, where she was a self-described "clothes lover—always." While she's worn gowns and dresses from almost every major designer, lately she's been favoring looks by Lanvin, Balenciaga, and Chloé. "And Ralph Lauren always has pieces every season that are right for my life," she says. A recent trip to Paris with the kids resulted in only one hour of shopping at Lanvin and Colette. "But I did well in an hour—and I wasn't late." Meanwhile, L.A. life has definitely had an effect on her personal style. "I was much more conservative in the way I dressed before I got to L.A.," she says. "I would never have worn a low-cut dress in Alabama. And of course, now I have no idea how to dress in East Coast weather. I was wearing boots with gowns when it snowed in New York the night of a black tie—while my girlfriends would be in stilettos and no stockings!"

Back in Los Angeles and happily ensconced in their adored home, the Tisch family still travels—spending a good part of the summer every year in Aspen, Colorado, and taking frequent trips to New York and Europe. "But L.A. is really home," says Jamie. "The year we spent in New York I missed our house and our yard. Especially with three small kids. We lived in a hotel for a year. They want to go out and play in the yard! And you know? So do I!"

Previous page: Jamie Tisch in her garden, dressed casually yet elegantly in a Tory by TRB tunic and Gucci pants. The house was designed by the great L.A. architect Paul Williams, who through the years designed residences for such members of Hollywood royalty as Zsa Zsa Gabor, Danny Thomas, and Barbara Stanwyck. He also created Frank Sinatra's swank bachelor pad and Lucille Ball's Palm Springs getaway.

After deciding that they needed a little extra room, Jamie and Steve recently had architect Marc Appleton add the new pool house, incorporating elements of the original home design. The pool is refurbished in iridescent blue ceramic tile.

Jamie and Steve bought the property, which sits on nine acres in Beverly Hills, in 1996 and spent several years remodeling, adding the charming ivy-covered porch off of the living room, which has views of the landscaping done by Jamie's good friend—and hair guru—Art Luna (the Tisches were his first clients).

Ed Ruscha's *A Blvd. Called Sunset* stands out in the dining room, hanging on chocolate/raspberry-colored walls done by painter Scott Flax. The candelabra chandelier came from Gianni Versace's apartment in Milan and on the far wall is a small painting by Georgia O'Keeffe.

In the Tisches' living room, an Irish mahogany console stands above basket weave ottomans that Jamie found in the Hamptons. An Edward Hopper watercolor hangs behind Italian candlesticks turned into lamps.

Jamie and Steve's art collection consists of blue chip contemporary artists: in the living room a Howard Hodgkin painting hangs over the fireplace, Ed Ruscha's *Able Moving Hearts* is on the back wall at left, and a Francesco Clemente painting can be seen over the vintage rolltop desk.

The Tisches converted the former guesthouse into a screening room worthy of Oscar winner Steve and now host screenings almost every week. Good friend Malisa Shriver painted the "Hollywood" screen cover with a Ruscha painting in mind. The rich leather club chairs from Hoffman are adorned with blue tapestry fabric cushions from Ralph Lauren and the crème chenille sofas are reproductions of similar pieces that Coco Chanel had in her Paris apartment. A brilliant David Hockney painting hangs over the fireplace, and *50th*, which Jamie commissioned for Steve's fiftieth birthday from Ed Ruscha himself, hangs in the back hallway.

An enchanting sitting room near the kitchen is luminous with hand-stenciled walls, a custom-made cherry desk from James Jennings, and a bench from Brenda Antin. Hand-embroidered drapes feature a floral design based on seventeenth- to nineteenth-century textiles, by Jed Johnson's company Chelsea Editions. The small picture is by German artist Oscar Bluhm.

The Tisches' home has a Hollywood who's who of former owners: Freddie Fields and Polly Bergen, Bill Cosby, and Michael Landon, to name just a few. Refinished walnut floors, original intricate crown moldings, and a baby grand piano add elegance to the home's entry. Jamie spotted the vintage center table in the home of friend and interior designer Tim Corrigan and convinced him that it would be perfect in her entry. *Chrysanthemum* by celebrated British painter Howard Hodgkin hangs just inside the dining room.

Shaun Caley Regen is a classic Hollywood fish-out-of-water story on two counts: she runs an art gallery, Regen Projects, in a town where what entertains people tends to be highly kinetic and a tad more superficial, and she lives in a minimalist Neutra house in a lushly Mediterranean neighborhood in West Hollywood, surrounded not by other Neutras and modernists, but by classic old Hollywood Spanish-style duplexes.

Regen and her late husband, Stuart Regen, purchased the house over eight years ago. (They were the third owners—it was originally built for the Miller family and is known in Neutra circles as the "Miller in Residence House.") The house appealed to them as the rare Neutra closer to their West Hollywood gallery than the Neutra-filled neighborhoods of Los Feliz and Silverlake. (Stuart, son of New York gallery owner Barbara Gladstone, was an L.A. art dealer and also the producer of the Oscar-winning *Leaving Las Vegas,* which he himself developed solely after discovering John O'Brien's obscure novel. He died in 1998 after a long struggle with non-Hodgkins lymphoma.)

Before she was Shaun Caley Regen, art gallerist, she was Shaun Caley, would-be novelist, editor of a Milan-based art magazine, West Coast editor of *Harper's Bazaar,* and all-around L.A.

groovy girl—a female type not common on the West Coast: she's edgy, she smokes, she's got long black gypsy hair (not a touch of blonde), and she's known for an aesthetic more New York or European than Los Angeles, although she claims to love her sun-drenched hometown as much as any beach bunny. Her style is decidedly East Coast glamour girl, with a touch of West Coast devil-may-care thrown in: Missoni sweaters, clingy pantsuits, high Louboutin heels, long scarves, and a sophisticated touch of bling in diamond earrings and a Buccellati ring. It's a look you wouldn't commonly see on actresses, agents, studio chiefs, or your average Hollywood D-Girl, but as L.A.'s top art dealer, Regen is really cut from her own hybrid cloth.

Her home is its own semihybrid as well: modern with touches of Mediterranean. The modernist clean angles of the house were obscured by greenery before the couple restored the landscaping to the purism integral to Neutra. The ceilings are low and wooden (a telltale sign of the architect), and the furniture, appropriate and modern, in camel and smoke hues. "I buy it all from Skank World," says Regen, "but we added built-ins in the living room, à la Neutra."

She recently redid the kitchen, claiming, coolly, "Neutra was really crappy at kitchens. I'm all for maintaining Neutra and all of

The Miller in Residence House, as photographed by Julius Shulman in March 1953. Regen and her husband were careful to retain the original integrity of Neutra's design when refurbishing the house.

that, but I'm also all for improvising for function, if necessary. I tried to deal with the kitchen in authentic Neutra style—but I couldn't really cook in it, and I love to cook here." She added high-tech appliances and copied the cork floors of Neutra's Kaufman House in Palm Springs, "something they used a lot in the fifties." Much of the rest of the house still maintains gray wall-to-wall carpeting, with one striking stand-out and ode to the movie biz: an object that looks like an Oscar statuette. "Stuart's mother bought us that," she laughs, "when *Leaving Las Vegas* didn't get nominated for Best Picture."

Of course, the house has become a showcase for many of Regen's stable of artists. The gallery was among the first to show Damien Hirst, Matthew Barney, Jack Pierson, and Richard Prince. There are paintings by John Currin, Lari Pittman (a teacher at UCLA who's becoming an influential L.A. artist), and a painting of the White Stripes' Meg White by Elizabeth Peyton.

Local naysayers were sure that when her husband passed away, Regen would never be able to keep the popular gallery going. Instead, she's become the art thorn in the side to New York–Beverly Hills gallery owner Larry Gagosian. Regen has helped launch L.A. artists Catherine Opie and Liz Lamer to international stardom, while maintaining West Coast representation of international art stars Currin, Prince, and Anish Kapoor. She sells to bigtime local collectors like CAA's Beth Swofford (who's been mentioned in *ARTnews* as one of the top two hundred art collectors in the world), Jacqui Getty, and Pam Levy, and Regen helps program California-based art projects such as the High Desert Test Sites, an annual exhibition of site-specific art.

"People might say that I'm not your typical Angeleno," Regen says, puffing on her cigarette, with an air of urbanity and sophistication—and a little European world weariness—not often associated with L.A. life. "But they also said nobody in Los Angeles would ever take art seriously." She's proved them wrong on both accounts.

Previous page: Regen's home is full of pieces by the most important contemporary artists, like *Pat* (1996), an oil on canvas by art-world darling John Currin that hangs in the entry foyer. Below sits a minimal wood bench designed by the Dutch gallery artists de Rijke/de Rooij for a film installation that was done at Regen Projects.

Shaun and Stuart purchased the jewel box–like Neutra home in 1996. Today she enjoys entertaining small groups of friends for impromptu dinners.

Drawings by gallery artist and good friend Raymond Pettibon are scattered over the chic yet understated master bedroom walls.

Regen meticulously maintained all of Neutra's original work, like the paneled wood ceiling and built-in wood cabinets. She added a whimsical Rietveld Zig Zag chair (at left), above which hangs an Alighiero Boetti drawing mounted on canvas. A portrait by Elizabeth Peyton of the White Stripes' Meg White can be seen on the far wall. Visible through the windows is the outdoor environment that landscape architect Jay Griffiths designed about five years ago, "working with the original plans, but augmenting them," says Regen. "He used the Modernism and geometry of the house all of the way to the street, making the interior yard more lush—after Rousseau."

Regen has an air of urbanity
and sophistication—and a little
European world weariness—
not often associated with L.A. life.

In addition to the original built-in sofa,
every element in Regen's charming
living room feels as though it was
made specifically for that very space,
like the Charles and Ray Eames
cowhide chair and glass-topped Isamu
Noguchi coffee table. A Charles Ray
black and white photo series from
1973 hangs above the sofa and James
Welling's green *Degrade, IGRE* (2001),
sits on the bookcase. The faux flea
market Oscar statue was a gift from
Stuart's mother, New York art dealer
Barbara Gladstone, when *Leaving
Las Vegas* was not nominated for an
Academy Award.

Neutra's camel table—original to the house—looks flawless in Regen's dining room, coupled with Thonet chairs from the late 1940s. A black leather Eames lounge chair with matching ottoman stands out near the fireplace, which includes the aluminum wood storage bin that is an iconic Neutra feature.

Though Regen owns some of the most valuable contemporary art around, one of her most treasured pieces is *Stuart & Gordo* (1996) by Billy Sullivan—a painting of her husband, Stuart Regen, and their dog, which hangs in the home office. Below that is an Aalto chair stacked with art. The small white side table is by Eero Saarinen, above which leans a painting by Stefan Hirsig, *Suspicious Mind I* (2004).

Downer (2003), a painting by young up-and-coming artist Francesca Gabbiani, hangs on the wall above the banquette.

The red leather banquettes and table were added when Regen renovated the kitchen with plans by Amy Murphy, who based her designs on Neutra's original kitchen. Joseph Beuys's black and white photograph *Coyote: I Like America and America Likes Me* (1974), rests on the table.

Interesting mementos along with significant works of art dot the large built-in bookcase in the library/guest suite of the house. A pen-and-ink on paper by Rosemarie Trockel, a black and white photograph by Susan Grayson, and a cast aluminum piece by Jenny Holzer are mixed with a bondage photo from the 1950s, which uber-artist Richard Prince found at a flea market and gave Regen as a gift.

As one half of the team who created Juicy Couture, the sportswear company that brought the ultimate L.A. lifestyle to the rest of the world, Pamela Skaist-Levy has pretty much the ultimate L.A. life. Married with a five-year-old son, she works her Juicy butt off at the company's Pacoima factory every day with her large team, then goes home to a gorgeous Beverly Hills house that she and her husband, Jef, recently redid. But on the weekends, every weekend—like New Yorkers and Londoners but not like most Angelenos—she and the family retreat to a fabulous Malibu beach house that is the perfect combination of beachy and haute, collectibles and casual, stark and colorful. In that way it's much like the empire of Juicy sweats, sweaters, and classics she and partner Gela Taylor have created.

Levy grew up in what was once known as Orange County, known more recently as "the O.C."—so she's no stranger to the Southern California surf-and-skate culture. "We grew up body boarding, skateboarding. Finally I learned how to surf. And I could have become a full-blown surf rat, I was so bitten by the bug. I can never get enough beach."

So once Juicy exploded, a house in Malibu was definitely in the cards—but Levy and her husband (a film producer) were very spe-cific about what they wanted. According to Levy, they spent two not-all-that-patient years looking for "a really romantic cottage on the beach. They're not so easy to find; people tear them down. Those original Malibu cottages don't exist anymore. There are just a few one-story cottages with high ceilings. You drive down the Colony and see full-blown monstrosities. And for us, a yard was very important. Our Malibu house had to have a huge deck."

But even after locating what they deemed "the ideal house," they encountered another hurdle: it wasn't for sale. Jef Levy began pestering the owner. Turned out he was a European talk-show host—the Johnny Carson of Germany—and was rarely there. Finally, they made him an offer he couldn't refuse.

Now the couple's been heading out to "the Bu" every Friday to Sunday for the last three years, even in the midst of some of L.A.'s rainier winters. "The beach inspires me every weekend," Levy says. "It clears my mind and makes me able to dream and create. And if you want to be social, there's a huge social life in Malibu. Even in the winter, there's a nice community. We go to Nobu every weekend, early, and we always bring Noah. And we'll go to Tony's Taverna. And of course, I live in Juicy, morning, noon, and night. When it's cold, I'll throw a cashmere sweater over my Juicy sweats." (In town, it's more about Lanvin dresses and Birkin bags.)

Levy may know her fabrics, but when it came to the house, she employed the furniture wisdom of Brenda Antin, a decorator and head of an L.A. dynasty that includes sons Steven Antin, a writer, and Jonathan Antin, a well-known hairdresser with his own name-sake salon. (Jef Levy produced the movie *Inside Monkey Zetterling,* which Steven Antin wrote.) "I went to Brenda's shop on Beverly Boulevard," says Pam, "and in her store she had such beautiful things—she's got an amazing eye. I saw this turquoise chair and a Portuguese hutch from the early 1900s, and I knew that was exactly how I wanted to do my house."

The Levys' house was built in the 1940s and is one of Malibu Colony's original cottages. You enter through a courtyard loaded with bougainvillea on both sides like a canopy, and on the left is a small guesthouse—cozy, decorated like the rest of the house, and the frequent summer weekend home to Gela and her husband, Duran Duran's John Taylor. It contains a chandelier that Pam and Gela—the self-dubbed and often similarly dressed and tressed "P&G"— found during the couture shows in Paris. "We call it 'Lady Beach Shack,'" says Pam.

"And the look of the house is very 'Brenda,'" she points out. "The white on the walls is more Colonial than nautical. But white is a theme. I broke it up with a zebra rug, turquoise art glass, huge orange pillows, and orange Hermès throws. The palette came from that one chair I saw in Brenda's shop. She designed most of the furniture herself. And this house looks nothing like our house in town. That's very midcentury modern, built in 1958, sort of James Bond zen. It's kind of the ultimate party pad."

But then, the Malibu house has also become party central—it's just that it's "family party central." All manner of kids come over and the Levys do clam bakes and lobster at five thirty, then go to sleep early and get up early.

The turquoise art glass strewn about the house is one of the many ways the outdoors—the ocean's hue—is brought indoors. "I started collecting art glass a long time ago," says Levy. "When I was on bed rest when pregnant with Noah, I was on eBay collecting art glass all the time. I also got some from the store Retro on LaBrea—some is Murano, some is Blanco, some pieces are valuable—and some are worthless."

Even the art on the walls of the Malibu house, most bought under the watchful eye of gallery owner and art consultant Shaun Caley Regen, refers to the beach: two photographs by Catherine Opie, classic surf photos from Don James's "Surfing San Onofre to Point Dume" series, pictures Levy collected long before they had the place because "I always knew I would have a Malibu house." Two large abstracts by hot German artist Wolfgang Tillmans in the bedroom were also purchased from Regen's gallery, "which my pal Jacqui Getty took me to. She brought me to the Wolfgang Tillmans show, I remember. I didn't know he did big abstracts."

The house deceptively has more room than it appears from the outside: there are two bedrooms, plus a loft bedroom above the living room, and the guesthouse.

And then there is arguably the most important part of the house: its outdoor areas. Pam and Jef expanded the patio farther out than what one of its previous owners, Dot Spiking, had done. A trellis covered in bougainvillea shades an enormous outdoor dining table and patio floors in their original wood. There are large chocolate-colored umbrellas outside, and the deck furniture, in chocolate and white, adorns both the bottom level deck and the upper deck. "If you want to be social in Malibu," says Pam, "you sit on the upper deck and wave to people." The downstairs deck also has two couches, monogrammed chocolate cushions, and a wicker coffee table that Brenda Antin painted with black marine paint. "This is our living room and our dining room in the summer. No one stays in the house. That's why we have so many umbrellas."

This doesn't mean that the petite, pale blonde gets—God forbid —tan. "When I surf, I cover my whole body with zinc," she says. "When I do my eight-mile beach walks, I put on a long T-shirt, sun-block my hands, and pop on a Juicy beach hat. Sometimes I go with Noah, sometimes with a group of girls. That's what Malibu is about. We bike-ride every day, we walk to the tide pools. And I get to not think about clothes at all."

As Juicy expands into shoes and branches out in retail, and the busier Pam and Gela become, the more the Malibu house becomes a kind of retreat from the Levys' demanding and fast-paced L.A. lives. "Spending this much time here has made me want to do a Juicy surf line—but I need the time," Pam says. "There just never seems to be enough time!"

Previous page: Pam and Noah chill out in the master bedroom of the 1940s Malibu beach cottage. She sparkles in an emerald Imitation of Christ dress and vintage necklace.

The original brick fireplace warms the living room and a ladder leads up to the charming guest sleeping loft. Levy's son asked, "Did you kill that animal, Mama?" referring to the ten-foot-long custom zebra bench and matching footstool by the window. Adding to the eccentric mix are orange Hermès throws and pillows.

The living room has the perfect laid-back beach vibe: a simple white denim covered couch designed by Antin, a tray of turquoise French milk goblets, and ocean blue lamps. A nineteenth-century Portuguese hutch adds a dash of exotic elegance, as does an antique Turkish Oushak carpet.

Opposite: A custom-made ebony wood table with marble top and black wicker chairs adorn the dining room. Levy wanted everything to be "luxurious but comfortable—and machine washable!" The two framed photos of surfers are from the well-known series "Surfing San Onofre to Point Dume" (1936–1942), by Don James.

The loft bedroom was added by the home's former owners, Barry and Dot Spikings, and boasts the most amazing views on the property. The Malibu house serves as a refuge of casual weekend living away for Pam, Jef, and their four-year-old son Noah's hectic L.A. lives.

The custom-made chocolate couches with monogrammed cushions and wicker table serve as the Levys' dining and living rooms during the summer. Just beyond, on the upper deck, they can lounge in the sun and watch people cruise by on the beach.

Four-year-old Noah races for the camera in his pirate gear as Levy stands watch, in an elegant Chloé suit and Juicy Couture tank.

A charming trellis, covered with bougainvillea, shelters a table for twelve on the outside lower deck with its expansive ocean views.

Opposite page: A view through the house from the master bedroom. The floors are natural wood with a five-inch white border in every room. The second in a pair of Wolfgang Tillmans' photographs hangs above a white denim couch warmed by an orange Hermès throw over the arm.

Built in the 1940s, the house is one of the original cottages on the beachside in the Colony. Levy calls the white wood "more Colonial than nautical." The open wood-beamed kitchen is perfect for the casual entertaining they do in "the Bu." Here in the kitchen and displayed throughout the house are pieces from her extensive turquoise glass collection.

A study in contrasts: in the master bedroom a zebra print bench sits at the foot of an airy "Guinevere" carved Colonial canopy bed, always covered in Frette sheets. Levy acquired the abstract Wolfgang Tillmans photos on the wall from Shaun Caley Regen.

Somehow Levy pulls off the chandelier in the bathroom (far right), making it look hip and incredibly chic. Carol Abbott, who oversaw the project, completely renovated the master bath. Carrera marble adds a classic touch.

Levy's closet reflects her "Juicy life" and style: Juicy terry sweats, straw hats, and Vans sneakers next to a collection of Hermès Birkin bags. She has a passion for Louis Vuitton hard cases, Prada cashmere, and Manolo flats. At the beach she's into an "eclectic mix of laid-back surf/skate clothes, Hollywood glamour, vintage and full-blown comfort," she says. "Have fun, be yourself, and never take it all too seriously."

Buying his Bel Air manse four years ago was a big gamble for entrepreneur Reagan Silber—but like many of his other high-stakes gambles, he turned it into a goldmine.

Back in 2000, the Texas trial lawyer and telecommunications pioneer owned a Dallas home and a New York apartment and was starting to consider a West Coast outpost, just for the sake of jet-setting and investment. "But I didn't think I would like L.A.," says Silber. "I hadn't been in New York for long—maybe three years—but I was already a New York snob. I'm just a really diligent, ambitious, disciplined guy, and I didn't think the L.A. life would suit me."

He purchased his current Bel Air home and planned to do only limited renovation. But then September 11, 2001, occurred—changing his outlook on pretty much everything. He promptly sold his New York and Dallas homes and hired New York–based architect Charles Allem to do a mega-renovation in Bel Air. (Silber feels that "in fifteen years, Charles Allem will be considered one of the major influences in modern architecture.") South African–born Allem is notorious for demanding his autonomy and not allowing clients to micromanage the design process. The renovation lasted for a full sixteen months. "Within minutes of meeting Charles, I knew that like any good relationship, it automatically works and you instantly understand each other—or you don't. It was great. I knew it was crazy—but I gave his firm an almost unlimited budget. And they blew right through it and exceeded it. But the end result worked."

Luckily for Silber, so have his L.A.-based business ventures. He's an investor in an indie movie production company named Plum Pictures; he created EdgeTV, a twenty-four-hour gaming entertainment channel devoted to games of "skill, strategy, and chance" (read: poker), and he's opening a W Hotel and Casino for Starwood on twenty-two acres of undeveloped farmland in Vegas in 2008. "It was like meeting the perfect storm when I found out Starwood wanted to do casinos," Silber says. "I got very, very fortunate with this opportunity. My land is near Peter Morton's Hard Rock Casino, and the casino Brad Pitt and George Clooney are creating—all off the strip. I think we will all really help each other."

Silber—who's morphed into something of a poker-playing wunderkind himself—hosted one of the first of the celeb-heavy poker-for-charity events at the house, attended by Leonardo DiCaprio, Tobey Maguire, David Schwimmer, Jack Black, Ellen DeGeneres, Sean Hayes, Heather Graham, Paul Rudd, and many others, organized by Amanda Scheer Demme for *GQ* magazine. Silber now hosts what others refer to as the "Billionaire Boys' Game" once a month. The stakes start at ten thousand dollars a hand, and it's about as far from a backroom poker game as you could ever get. Tobey Maguire (who's on the board of EdgeTV) and Leo DiCaprio are fixtures, as are good wines, excellent catering, and a smattering of Hollywood power players from all ilks.

"I really don't know how I fell into the whole gaming arena," confesses Silber. "I always played poker as a kid—we did it in my family. The whole thing just turned into a good confluence of opportunities. People started calling me in L.A. to play and I'm good at it. If you're willing to play a high-stakes game, it's a small world of people who will play at that level. And, like anything else, it's hard to go backwards. It's hard to drink light beer after beer or Diet Coke after Coke. You get used to the rush. Poker does seem to feed into the addictive nature of people in L.A.: it's the right combination of luck and skill. The best person doesn't always win —kinda like life. It's enough like life to make it truly interesting."

The same can be said for his larger-than-life modern house. When the feedback gives way to superlatives such as "mono-lithic" and "007-like," Reagan laughs. "I don't think that's right," he argues. "I think of it as more sophisticated, and not so tricked-up. I know it has some high-tech elements. I like to think of it as more design sophisticated. That's just my taste. To me, it's very mascu-line. The goal was to make it feel like I am living inside a piece of sculpture. I like masculine—and the challenge of contemporary architecture is to make it feel warm. I've been heading in this modern direction design-wise for about ten years now. But it's not a big cement void."

Indeed, Charles Allem's attention to detail—mink chairs, silver-tipped couches, textured walls, and the use of plush indoor furniture outdoors—warm up a potentially steely modern space. "I didn't exactly ask for those details," Silber offers. "I wouldn't have known to do mink chairs or silver tips on the bottom of the legs of couches. But I am detail-oriented, and it's not just for show. I actually live in this house, my office is in this house, and it's become a frequent gathering place, which I also love."

Aside from the poker events, Silber hosts Democratic Party fund-raisers and consciousness-raising events at his home, and will entertain at least once a month, hosting around fifty to seventy-five people on his third-floor outdoor deck, with "tons of grilled food, passed food, frozen drinks—and with the reflection on the pool, it's perfect. Another thing I'll do is entertain twenty-five outside on the main living level with cocktail parties. And people get a real kick out of touring the house. They like to walk through every room. I'm happy in this house. If I met a girl and decided to get married, I'd stay in it—it's very livable, even with children. It's not a big crazy place you can't live in.

"Nobody is more shocked than me that L.A. has really become my home," he sighs. "I never would have believed it. I still love New York, but I will never live there again. I've fallen for the lifestyle and entertaining and work of L.A., and now the casino project will keep me on the West Coast. It's a big enough, exciting enough project. Depending on how this goes, I think I will go into real estate development and the gaming business."

There's only one element in his home that reminds Reagan Silber of his Texas days: Warhol pieces that he purchased in Dallas of the Kennedy family. "I love the whole Kennedy motif," he says. "It ties back to my Texas roots. The Kennedy assassination ties back to Texas, and Democratic politics, pop art, and growing up in the sixties. These things all refer to my roots." Charles Allem advised on some of the rest of the art, like the Henry Moore piece, further proof of Silber's obsession with things sleek and modern.

Counteracting his infatuation with the cool and clean is his affection for his Labradoodle puppy and his undeniable, big passion for sports, especially golf. But contrary to what most others in Los Angeles might think, Reagan Silber does not believe he's living the ideal life.

"I wouldn't mind being Tiger Woods," he jokes. "And who wouldn't? He gets to play golf all the time, and," says the well-known bachelor about town (at least at this writing), "he's got a beautiful Swedish wife. Whose life could be better than his?"

Many of Silber's friends would repeat the same refrain about him.

Previous page: Silber's home office is done in red lacquered wood paneling and is duplexed with a stainless-steel staircase. The Andy Warhol lithographs behind the desk are from an eleven-piece series about the assassination of John F. Kennedy titled "The Dark Days in Dallas, November 22, 1963."

James Bond immediately comes to mind when you step up to the brushed satin stainless-steel entrance and doors that automatically open with a fingerprint scan. The custom-designed glass pyramid peeks out from above and as the doors whisk back, you are struck by the floor-to-ceiling views of Bel Air and Westwood.

Continuous stainless-steel panels create a fluid sculpture wall around the entry and sides of the property. Coupled with the ficus hedges behind them, the panels extend around the perimeter and shroud the house in privacy.

"The goal was to make it feel like I am living inside a piece of sculpture."

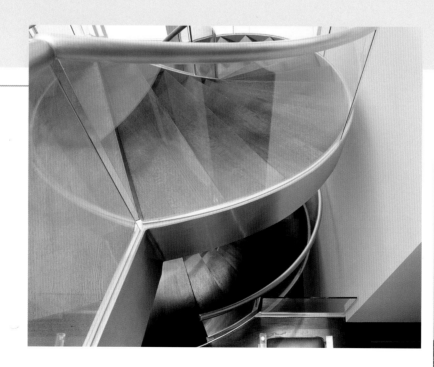

The stainless-steel floating staircase had to be craned in through the ceiling. The arm rail is made up of one continuous piece of metal.

The grand custom-built stainless-steel staircase is freestanding and looks as if it floats from floor to floor. Entertaining expert Colin Cowie designed the center table with its brown leather pedestal and aluminum top, above which sits a Daum amethyst sculpture. Three abstract paintings done in gray lead by American artist David Roth hang over a vintage Paul Frankl embossed green pony-skin curved chaise.

South African designer Charles Allem used many shades of green in the decor to match the lush exterior landscaping, like the mohair chairs with leather piping in this upstairs living room. The console is from Allem's personal collection and the sculpture *Wind Blown Hair* is by Hagenauer. The trellis outside (visible in the center background) covers a built-in terrazzo banquette and fire pit that are highlights when Silber entertains.

The central focus of this living room is the Paul Lazlo curved brown leather sofa that was previously owned by Francis Ford Coppola. Again, Allem used luxury materials with these 1950s Rafael chairs, which he reupholstered in green calfskin leather and mink to match the green mink pillows on the couch. The Modern One coffee table holds a chrome BIR sculpture from 1960.

The media room's unique striped brown wood and stainless-steel-paneled walls, custom designed by Allem, are its most striking feature. The amethyst Oom Grand Swivel Lounge chairs are perfect to relax in for one of Silber's movie screenings. The small stools are designed in green ostrich, wood, and stainless steel.

During dinner, Silber can enjoy stunning unobstructed views that stretch from downtown Los Angeles all the way to Catalina Island. Very avant-garde green mohair chairs with brown leather piping surround a Wenge wood table, another of Allem's designs. An Adam Fuss photogram from 1988 hangs on the wall. Outside, a terrace extends the length of the house.

The front windows of the home offer a view of the white terrazzo and grass checkerboard courtyard, which was formerly the driveway. Ficus trees encircle the property, enclosing a planter full of iceberg roses. A white leather and Lucite J. Robert Scott chair sits in the window.

Even the gym was custom designed by L.A. fitness guru Mark Harigian. In keeping with the use of luxury materials, all of the equipment was made from chocolate brown leather and stainless steel, and the walls are covered in suede.

Every material used and piece of furniture displayed, down to the Pratesi linens here in the master bedroom, was chosen with a very precise vision by Allem. He paid meticulous attention to details like the custom-made silk Bradbury wall upholstery with brown and green stitching. The overall feeling is very masculine, with a pair of matching embossed crocodile and stainless-steel nightstands that frame the custom-made bed. Lynn Weinberg designed the brown silk chaise, circa 1960.

Silber had to move a huge amount of land for the pool to sit where it does today. The sculpture is by Christopher Georgesco, an artist from Palm Springs.

The master bathroom features an oversized steam shower.

Shriftman shares a laugh with friends while entertaining at home, dressed in one of her favorite designers, Peter Som.

No one would dispute that New York transplant Lara Shriftman leads one of L.A.'s more colorful lives. Her high-flying PR company Harrison and Shriftman is bicoastally busy staging stylish events for clients like Mercedes, Motorola, Jimmy Choo, Sergio Rossi, Gwen Stefani's L.A.M.B clothing line, author Gigi Levangie Grazer, Juicy Couture, and Delman shoes. She single-handedly reinvented the idea of networking as a young blonde power PR girl in New York in the '90s (launching the term "Power PR Girl" by sheer force of her enthusiasm), then relocated to Los Angeles, reinvigorating the city's formerly sluggish social scene with her birthday parties and eclectic soirees. Her company's credited with inventing the promotional goodie bag (getting products into the hands of A-listers), and there's no doubt some connection in the fact that her closest friends are among the coolest L.A. eclectica: power agents, actors, designers, producers, scenesters extraordinaire. The L.A. social scene has become less homogenized since her energetic and ambitious arrival a few years ago. Not only that, it's thinner—she single-handedly put the colonic retreat spa, We Care, on the map, inviting pals like Casey and Ben Affleck to check it out. Half of Hollywood followed up.

In her own Hollywood Hills house, purchased in 2004 and decorated with the help of former Ian Schrager head architect Tim Andreas, the decor is the opposite of colorfully frenetic and kinetic: purposefully muted, an intentional bastion of serenity. Almost every room is clean, sleek, and white, except for Shriftman's Wedgwood-style dining room, which has black walls and a white border, and a black and white sunroom with yellow accents.

"This is the first project Tim's done on his own after eight years with Ian Schrager," Shriftman says. "After years of living primarily in New York," says the still bicoastal Shriftman, who's growing more L.A. passionate all the time, "I wanted the house to be white, clean, modern. The Delano, Ian Schrager's hotel in Miami Beach, is one of my favorite hotels in the world—that's what inspired me."

It makes sense that Shriftman would be turned on by the Delano: its white-hot modern decor set a new standard in the international language of groovy hotels in the mid-1990s. With its radical design, it self-consciously created a new social order of people who work in the media/entertainment/fashion axis, and travel among New York, Los Angeles, Miami, the Hamptons, and London as if they were all suburbs of one teeming Megalopolis of Media. As someone who's hosted events in all these outposts, it's a world she knows well. She helped create it and continues to market to it.

But Shriftman's L.A. house is more of a personal haven than an obvious party central. "I tend to entertain for about five to twenty people at home," says the coauthor, with New York partner Elizabeth Harrison, of two books: *Fête Accompli! The Ultimate Guide to Creative Entertaining* and *Fête Accompli! The Ultimate Party Planning Guide*. Her home soirees have included Serena Williams's birthday and a party for Chris Heinz (son of Teresa Heinz Kerry). Indeed, the fragile factor—white fur blankets on the couch in the living room, two white leather chairs by Milo Baughman (from his store on La Cienega), white curtains, crystal-beaded lamps—makes the idea of tons of people trooping through rather prohibitive. "I do that for a business," says Shriftman. "I don't need to do that at home."

One part of the house that's geared for guests is the sunroom, with its smattering of sunny yellow accents like lamps, and a whole collection of yellow-spined first-edition Nancy Drew books, "a present from a friend" who knows Shriftman's predilection for no-nonsense Nancy, a girl likewise so shrewd nothing escapes her eagle-eye powers of observation.

The sunroom reflects the influence of a couple of Laurens: Ralph Lauren, whose furnishings Shriftman loves ("my whole New York apartment is chocolate brown Ralph Lauren"), and his nephew Greg, whose paintings hang over two Ralph Lauren daybeds. "Lara Flynn Boyle made this for me," notes Shriftman, pointing to a black sequin-covered ottoman. "And this is the best thing in my house: a huge disco ball, hanging from the center of the room. When it's dark, it reflects. I'm very much into light—and surprisingly, I'm way more of a day person than a night person, which is what everyone would expect me to be." Even so, it takes a certain kind of social animal to have a disco ball in her home.

The sunroom leads outside to Shriftman's big pool and outdoor living room setup: another great place for entertaining. There are yellow wicker chairs, a Moroccan table with wrought-iron chairs, deep blue glass cubes to set cold drinks on, and lanterns strewn up for nighttime entertaining. A white wood daybed offers relaxation, next to cushy Ralph Lauren navy and white checked and paisley pillows, which sit beside the pool.

The TV room adds one of the house's biggest splashes of color: large blue, black and white flowers cover the wallpaper, and a white rug with navy running through it draws the theme around the room.

A blue suede Knoll sofa (covered in Ralph Lauren fabric) really punches up the blue theme, contrasting with a black leather Ralph Lauren chrome sling chair that sits next to it. On the walls, a true touch of Hollywood: fashion sketches by designers Shriftman has worked with or knows, the beginnings of red carpet creations for the likes of Nicole Kidman, Gwyneth Paltrow, Halle Berry, and various other glamorous Hollywood women. No stranger to glam herself, Shriftman may enjoy the more "casz" L.A. dress code—but everything else about her grooming harkens back to the Hollywood glam days of yore: fully (and very full) tousled, well-maintained, multihued blonde tresses, perfectly buffed French toes, and a seamless not-too-done tan year-round. It's that effortless look that takes much effort but makes the New York transplant seem like an L.A. native.

The second floor has no remnants of the Hollywood life at all. Her master bedroom is a pastiche of clean white bedding and heavy wood furniture, with great views of the Hollywood Hills out the copious windows that lend more than a touch of green to the space. And as for the guest bedroom, with its needlepoint embroidered chairs from her grandmother—well, it's practically old-fashioned compared with the rest of the house. It seems as though the modernity of the rest of the house is for day, and her upstairs nighttime retreat reflects a feeling you don't hear about in the L.A. design world very often: cozy.

The house's real showcase may be the stunning dining room. With a tip of the hat to Fornasetti, its big, round white table features unmatched black and white chairs—each one different—complemented by matte black walls with bright white trim. "That's Tim's creation," Shriftman points out. "I would never have had the nerve to paint these walls black—but he insisted. He just knew it would work well in contrast to the rest of the house. The minute I saw it finished, I fell in love with it."

Shriftman's bright, modern, efficient kitchen leads the way to a tiny nook in the back, her home office. In contrast to the rest of house, its walls are painted Easter-egg pink, and the furniture painted a shiny black lacquer. "I cut a reference out of French *Vogue*," Shriftman laughs, pointing to a page of a Parisian dressing room that inspired her. "I figured, the one room I do my work in should probably be allowed to have color in it. You need that when you're planning parties, events, and marketing campaigns. But it's pretty much my one concession to New York in my L.A. house."

The spectacular all-glass sunroom opens onto a brick outdoor patio. A pair of Ralph Lauren brown linen and wicker chaise longues frame the door. The room also includes paintings by Ralph's nephew, L.A. artist Greg Lauren, as well as a beaded footstool (a past birthday gift) made by Shriftman's good friend Lara Flynn Boyle.

On the second floor, Shriftman's spacious all-white bedroom is a cozy retreat with killer views of the Hollywood Hills. Her uncle gave her the leather wing-backed chairs as a gift and above them hangs a painting by L.A. artist Patrick McCarthy.

Shriftman's L.A. house is more of a personal haven than an obvious party central.

With its clean white walls and crisp Italian white sofa, the living room exudes the perfect casual yet sophisticated L.A. style. Lara likes to feature work by good friends in her home, such as this glass coffee table from Minotti furniture designer Mary Ta in the center of the room; a color photograph by Tierney Gearon; and flowers from celebrity florist Eric Buterbaugh. The standing rattan Bolla lamps and classic mirror came from Italy.

The showstopper of the house may be its stunning dining room, with views of Beverly Hills and not-often-seen black matte walls, courtesy of interior designer Tim Andreas. The chairs are covered in unmatched Timney Fowler fabric and the table is set with Hermès china and flatware.

Shriftman favors the clean lines of a Ralph Lauren black leather and chrome sling chair, juxtaposed with big splashes of color from the floral wallpaper. Dozens of photographs with family and friends, as well as sketches by well-known fashion designers Shriftman has worked with, line the bookshelves.

Shriftman's patio and pool area is an oasis tucked away in the Hollywood Hills, with a Gervasoni daybed and custom-made white terry-cloth pillows. The cabana is perfect for laid-back entertaining and guests can check themselves out in the wicker mirror, a gift from Shriftman's parents.

Displayed in the chic sunroom is Shriftman's collection of first-edition Nancy Drew books (*The Clue of the Dancing Puppet, The Secret of Red Gate Farm*), a gift from automotive heir Jay Penske. Shriftman imported the standing Murano glass lamp from Andromeda, Italy.

Shriftman and her partner Elizabeth Harrison published *Fête Accompli* in 2004, detailing their secrets to Hollywood-style entertaining, including interviews with celebrities such as Diane von Furstenberg and Donald Trump.

Keith Addis and Keri Selig own a home that lives and breathes L.A. history. It is that history that first made them fall in love with it. The Spanish colonial, built in 1922 in the historic Los Feliz area, was inhabited by one of Los Angeles' most celebrated couples, philosophers Will and Ariel Durant, for over forty years. Authors of the Pulitzer Prize–winning book *The Story of Civilization,* the Durants were part of Los Angeles cognoscenti for many years (until their deaths in 1981, two weeks apart) and counted the likes of Charlie Chaplin, Bertrand Russell, Albert Einstein, George Bernard Shaw, and Clarence Darrow as friends. Seeing the potential of what the house again could be, Addis, a film and television producer and personal manager (his clients include Ted Danson, Sam Waterston, and Jeff Goldblum), and Selig, an independent producer with her own production company, Intuition Productions, were completely taken with it and were intent on doing everything possible to restore it to its original magnificence.

Though they never imagined living "that far east" in Los Angeles, Addis and Selig say that they now "can't imagine living anywhere else." The house (and the neighborhood) were really made for them: in addition to being steeped in history, the house has significant authentic California architecture, a fantastic view (on a clear day you can see as far west as the ocean), and lots of outdoor space (it sits on almost two acres). "It is almost impossible to find a place with land and a view. It is so rare," says Selig. The couple love the neighborhood for its great old houses, most of which were built in the 1920s, as well as the fact that the area is increasingly attracting more and more artists—painters, writers, directors, musicians, and so forth. The location is also a perfect fit for them because they simultaneously feel like they are away from the city yet right on top of it. "I drive through Hollywood every day constantly dealing with the reality of the city that we live in," says Addis. Only in Los Angeles can they have the juxtaposition of the grandeur and privacy their house affords, right in the heart of the city.

When they bought the house, it hadn't had much renovation in many years and Addis and Selig knew that they would have to restore it literally from the ground up. They replaced every single pipe wire (in 1922 wires were insulated with cloth!) in the house and completely gutted and rebuilt the entire irrigation system before they even started on the structural restoration.

Their contractor, Sam Schatz, did most of the restoration work, aided by an architect and historian who the couple hired. Because there was only one photograph of the house (reproduced on page 105) available to the couple when they started the restoration—a picture from the Durants' autobiography, taken in the 1950s—they made additions to the house "in the spirit of how we wished all of those details would have been handled when the house was originally built." They added a deck with a Jacuzzi around the pool. They also added a balcony, which required extending the roof, so without any of the original plans they looked to the house as their guide. "We matched all of the existing architectural details in everything that we did," says Addis. Always with the notion "that every change that we made should look like it was part of the original plan," they spent about a year restoring and remodeling before moving in May 2000.

Though they made the bulk of the interior design decisions themselves, the couple worked with designer Jenny Armit to pull their vision of the house together. Again taking their cue from the house itself and also drawing inspiration from a George Hurrell photograph they own, the couple wanted the interior to look as their version of Veronica Lake (the real one was a bit of a tragic figure) or someone like her that would have lived there in the forties. In other words, they sought old Hollywood glamour mixed with comfort and authenticity. They wanted every room to have warmth, not a museumlike feeling but the security and serenity of a home. "A great house has to have at least three fabulous places just to hang out and do nothing," says Addis. Though the couple loves both of their home offices and the gazebo they added for year-round outdoor dining, they seem to do most of their hanging out in the screening room, their bedroom, and the kitchen.

The home's furniture and lighting fixtures came from all over the world, as the couple made it a hobby to look for French or French-inspired 1940s Moderne furniture wherever they were. Their finds include the beautifully designed and fabricated cabinets that they discovered in New York and at the Marché aux Puces—the famous Parisian flea market (which is one of Addis's favorite places in the world). The draperies designed by Armit were made in England, "because she was so confident about the quality of the craftsmanship." Instead of using photo albums, their collection of arts and crafts serves as a really meaningful travel journal that documents the places they have been or the adventures they have had. They are crazy about the beautiful carving that hangs over their bed; it came from a Burmese temple and they found it in Bangkok. One of their favorite pieces is the Francis Picabia painting that hangs over the living room fireplace. Done in the late 1920s, the picture was the beginning of Addis's avid interest in Cubism.

Addis and Selig were also motivated by sources closer to home. Inspired by a rug he saw in a screening room at the historic Sunset Gower Studios, Addis worked with Jenny Armit to adapt the design for the rugs that are now in the living room and the sunroom. The sunroom was one of the biggest challenges in the house "to make comfortable." It needed to have furniture that you could relax on while allowing you to take full advantage of the views from all of the windows. A traditional sofa just would not work, so Addis and Selig had a banquette couch custom-made and modeled after something similar that was in a room in actor Jimmy Stewart's house. The couch is one of many homages to old Hollywood throughout the house.

One might think that the interesting hexagonal shape of the house would provide more of a decorating challenge than it was worth, but Addis and Selig have utilized the space incredibly well. They especially love their dining room; Selig says "it is fantastic because it accommodates a round dining table so when you have ten guests it makes it easier for everyone to talk to each other." They never have to worry about who sits next to whom—and why would they, when their aptly named Casa de la Vista regularly hosts some of the most interesting people in Los Angeles? Doing their very best to carry on the tradition of the Durants and their reputation for hosting eclectic dinner guests, Addis and Selig have hosted writers Harlan Ellison (*Twilight Zone, I, Robot*) and Michael Tolkin (*The Player*), actors Judy Davis and Peter Weller, producer Tracey Edmonds, and physicist Gentry Lee. No doubt, they have done the Durants proud.

Previous page: The old-world Hollywood glamour of the home is breathtaking, as evidenced here by the majestic sweeping staircase where a Van Caulaert framed poster of 1920s French actress Cécile Sorel hangs. Below, on the first floor is a 1953 black and white Dennis Stock photograph of Audrey Hepburn during the filming of *Sabrina*. Addis and Selig filled the house with French Deco pieces, like the console under the mirror at right and the Jules Leleu cabinet in the background, both from the 1940s.

Reading scripts is a weekly routine for producers Selig and Addis.

A family photograph of the home when Will and Ariel Durant were in residence.

The sunlit living room off of the foyer reflects the Spanish Colonial influence of the home. The couches and square coffee table were fabricated in Los Angeles in 2001 to match the original French pieces in the home. The heavy velvet drapes were designed by Jenny Armit, who collaborated with Addis and Selig on much of the interior design.

Many of the original elements from 1922 still exist in the grand double-height foyer, such as the curved wood door with inlaid stained glass, the stained-glass panels, and wrought-iron railing running up the staircase (which the previous owners had painted red and gold). French pieces abound, from the red velvet couch—a French Deco reproduction, to the Picassoesque bronze lamp on the side table and the 1940s Lalique glass lamp adjacent to the front door.

The hexagonal-shaped sunroom was built with the house in 1922 and retains the original Craftsman tile. The custom-made banquette couch was modeled after a 1940s photograph of a room in Jimmy Stewart's residence.

Two chairs designed by Jenny Armit frame the sunroom entrance into the main salon. The chocolate suede chaise was custom-made and the French armoire by Desnos dates from 1939. The original Craftsman-influenced fireplace needed only slight restoration. The untitled Francis Picabia painting from 1929 hanging above the mantel is one of Addis and Selig's most prized possessions in their home. Bronze French wall sconces by Jean Percel, circa 1940s, flank the mantel.

The hexagonal-shaped office is original, but Addis and Selig had all of the windows enlarged while remodeling. The furniture and torchiere lamps were designed by Tom Rael and fabricated in Los Angeles.

On a clear day you can see all the way to the ocean from Addis and Selig's Los Feliz hills home.

The Durants entertained members of the intelligentsia like Albert Einstein and celebrities such as Charlie Chaplin in the stunning residence. Matching blue pieces of California pottery from the 1930s accent the original entrance.

Addis and general contractor Sam Schatz designed and added the portico with built-in fireplace and overhead heaters in 2004.

Bullard mixes traditional period pieces with contemporary elements from his own line. In the living room the dramatic items from Martynus-Tripp include an ebonized walnut table, as well as a sofa and chairs custom embroidered with red arabesques. Voluminous deep red silk Bugatti drapes hang next to an ancestral painting from 1730.

Famed interior designer Martyn Lawrence Bullard lives a true Hollywood story—though he likes to call it "Hollywood in reverse." A classically trained actor (Royal Academy of Dramatic Art and Lee Strasberg) and former model, Bullard came to Los Angeles from London about twelve years ago with the dream of becoming a famous movie star. Though things did not exactly go as planned, a role in the film *I Woke Up Early the Day I Died* (the last Ed Wood script ever written) led Bullard to the brilliant career he currently enjoys—designing spaces for the rich and famous.

The story goes like this: One of the producers of *I Woke Up Early the Day I Died,* Victor Ginsburg, had a company called Hollywood Film Works. One night, Bullard had Victor over to his house for dinner. "The place was a flea market fix-up," Bullard recalls. Victor loved what Bullard had done with his house so much that he asked him to do the Film Works offices. For the fun of it, and the possibility that he might get another film role out of the project, Bullard set to work. "I did the offices in a 'Casablanca goes to India via the flea market' vibe and spent about thirty thousand dollars, which is funny because that is what I spend on people's lamps nowadays."

The day the offices were finished Bullard received a phone call from Liz Heller, an executive at Capitol Records at the time. She told him she loved the Film Works offices and asked him to see what he could do with her house. Very sure to let her know that interior design was not really what he did for a living, Bullard nonetheless agreed to meet with her. He started to decorate her house right away. A few months later model Cheryl Tiegs had Bullard designing a Balinese pavilion in the hills of Bel Air. In true Hollywood fashion, within six months of the Tiegs project, Martyn Lawrence Bullard's interior designs were in or on the cover of six magazines around the world.

A star was born.

Though Bullard has no formal training in interior design, he has a good eye that he credits to his parents. As a child, he traveled extensively, which provided him with an early education in design. His father, an opera-singer-turned-businessman, and mother encouraged his fascination with history and the decorative arts, by taking him to see palaces, museums, and opera houses. It was the opportunity to take in all of these incredible sites from a very young age that he believes shaped his aesthetic as a designer.

In addition to endowing Bullard with a love for beautiful things, his father also encouraged Martyn's precocious energy by renting him a stall in London's famed Greenwich Antique Market at the age of twelve. He used to run around buying and selling silver spoons, decorative pots, and antique pins. "It is how I learned the antique industry," he says. The money he made, though originally pocket money, later supported him through drama school.

Fame has surrounded Bullard since he arrived in Los Angeles; the house he lives in now, the Villa Swanson, is the third in an incredible flow of historical Hollywood homes he has inhabited. His first house was built by Charlie Chaplin and was the dressing room for Norma Tallmadge. Later Lucille Ball and Judy Garland each called it home. Bullard's next residence was a house in the Hollywood Hills that had once belonged to Jim Morrison.

Villa Swanson came to him via friend and photographer Tim Street-Porter, who at the time was shooting Bullard's work at the Pepsi-Cola Ranch in Santa Fe for *Architectural Digest*. "Tim told me about the house on a Saturday, I flew back to see it on Sunday, and by Monday, I had bought it. I walked in and completely fell in love with it."

The totally "enchanted house" in a cul-de-sac of eight houses (which at one point had residents such as Raymond Navarro, Maurice Chevalier, costume designer Adrian, and Jean Harlow) in Whitley Heights has an old Hollywood romance to it that immediately struck a chord. The house was built in 1924 for a German silent movie director who never actually lived in it; its first inhabitant was Rudolph Valentino, who lived there while renovating his estate, Falcon Lair. Gloria Swanson lived in the house twice—once in the early 1930s and then again when she was filming *Sunset Boulevard*. William Faulkner lived in the house and used it as his writing pavilion in the late 1950s and early 1960s. Faulkner helped write the screenplay for *All About Eve* on the balcony off of Bullard's bedroom.

When Bullard bought the house in early 2003, though beautiful, it was in a bit of disrepair. He began a complete restoration replacing the damaged wood flooring with the wood from an old barn in Idaho and shipping in antique French limestone and terra-cotta for the patios. The restoration was not without wonderful surprises: He uncovered an original nineteenth-century floor in the kitchen that had been buried under 1980s Mexican tiles, and an arched breakfast nook that had been filled in with plaster and covered by a refrigerator. Most exciting of all, Faulkner had built-in bookcases in the living room during his residence, and when Bullard tore them down he discovered that they had hidden a third of the doorway into the dining room. Though he thinks he may have discovered all of the

villa's secrets, there is local legend of a remaining undiscovered Faulkner manuscript stashed around the house somewhere.

With clients and friends that range from royalty to pop stars to A-list celebrities, Bullard has made a name for himself the world over not only for his design but for his fabulous parties. With its four tiered gardens, hidden nooks, and seamless indoor/outdoor space, his home has served as the setting for many wildly fantastic themed soirees with celebs such as Mimi Rogers, Susanna Hoffs, shoe designers Christian Louboutin and Tamara Mellon, fashion designer Jasper Conran, and Christina Aguilera in attendance. "The house has always had a great Hollywood energy," Bullard says. Whitley Heights is known as one of the first Hollywood communities and Bullard is doing his very best to keep up the neighborhood's long tradition of fun, frivolity, and glamour.

When thinking about the interior decor, Bullard let the architectural style of the house be his guide. Wanting to enhance its inherent Mediterranean flavor, he collected and decorated mostly with eighteenth-century Spanish, Portuguese, and Italian furniture. There are pieces from auction houses in New York, Los Angeles, San Francisco, Paris, and London. There are a considerable number of Milanese pieces, a marvelous collection of ivory boxes with black penoir, and lots of coral spotted throughout the space. Bullard used the color red to unify the house and instill an authentic Spanish Mediterranean flavor. Lush red silk drapes and exotic red embroidery detail at the bottom of the sofa in the living room also give the house a touch of the Orient.

Influenced every day by what is around him, Bullard believes that interior design is all about the details. Though his personal taste leans to the exotic, Bullard has designed houses in an incredible number of diverse styles, such as a mod 1960s place for famed hair stylist Vidal Sassoon in London, a home with 1940s glamour for Christina Aguilera, a big Moroccan fantasy for music mogul Damon Dash, a Tuscan villa for Aaron Sorkin, and a Spanish Mediterranean villa for Ed Norton.

Despite the attention Martyn Lawrence Bullard pays in his work to the very beautiful and often very expensive, he says, "I don't believe that there should be anything in your house that you can't use, drink from, sit on, or eat out of." For him, comfort is the key to the enjoyment of a house. It is all about "living life, having fun, enjoying beautiful things, and loving living in Hollywood."

Bullard dresses casually at home in jeans and a T-shirt during his rare days off from designing and hosting celebrity segments on Britain's number one morning show, *This Morning*. He also has a new show on TLC called *Material World*, which takes a look behind the scenes of the design industry.

The villa has impeccable Hollywood credentials: the first occupant was film star Rudolph Valentino; it is where Gloria Swanson lived while filming *Sunset Boulevard;* and the home was later turned into a writing atelier for William Faulkner. With its overgrown landscaping, custom hand-embroidered Moroccan pillows, and various levels of daybeds with cushions, the terraced garden has the feeling of an exotic Casbah.

Much of the original kitchen was preserved and restored, including the brick floor and the vintage stove.

Bullard installed an eighteenth-century limestone fireplace in the living room, above which sits a mirror in a Peruvian frame that once held a painting of Madonna and child. Also on the mantel are pieces of coral and Victorian English silver ram horn candlesticks; Bullard jokes that they "reveal how distinctly Aries I really am!"

A charming alcove in the kitchen exemplifies the true Spanish design of the villa. An antique Indian table is paired with bone-inlaid Syrian hunting chairs and a Portuguese bench covered in black and white striped Manuel Canovas fabric. Nineteenth-century *ratablos,* images of Mexican icons, add color to the walls and a reproduction of the original light fixture illuminates the tableau.

The Portuguese bed made of jacaranda wood is dressed in custom Martynus-Tripp bedding topped with a nineteenth-century Scottish paisley cover and matching pillows.

Bullard's home certainly reflects his favorite Oscar Wilde saying, "All beautiful things belong to the same era." In the master bedroom, a seventeenth-century Andrea Saachi painting of a male slave hangs over the fireplace, next to a pair of Italian Sanguine study drawings.

Gloria Swanson had the original washbasin raised to accommodate her bad back in the enchanting mirrored master bath. The Moroccan lantern adds a bit of old-world charm.

The original heavy wood door from 1924 leads out to a charming ivy-covered loggia, where Bullard enjoys coffee in the morning. Eighteenth-century Turkish candlesticks and silver hammam bowls sit on a nineteenth-century tablecloth imported from Uzbekistan. The iron chairs are from the Baroness de Rothschild. Assorted Moroccan lanterns strewn about the terrace and a glass star fixture light the portico in the evenings.

Opposite: Villa Swanson is perfectly built for that indoor/outdoor life that L.A. residents love so much. Bullard's formal yet comfortable dining room opens onto a small court-yard featuring a fountain made from original 1920s Malibu tiles and a tree adorned with floating candles. A chandelier that once belonged to Gloria Swanson hangs from the ceiling. Nineteenth-century Venetian Blackamoors watch over the opulent ebony and inlaid ivory Milanese dining table and chairs from the eighteenth century. Bullard found the striking black and white rug in a souk in Marrakech.

When Bullard needs a respite from his glamorous, celebrity-fueled Hollywood life, he can relax in the calm elegance of the upstairs library. An antique French leather club sofa with silk velvet cushions is filled with assorted paisley pillows. The walls are covered with photographs from his extensive collection—works by Herb Ritts, Cindy Sherman, Peter Beard, Bruce Weber, and Horst to name a few—framed in decorative wood Martynus frames. Mid-nineteenth-century Syrian and Moroccan mother-of-pearl inlaid side tables are scattered around the room and sit on an ornate antique Turkish rug once belonging to L.A. design royalty Tony Duquette.

The flame appears to dance on sand in Rodkin's custom-built fireplace. A gold turn-of-the-century Victorian gilt column, topped with a seated Buddha from Bali, stands to the left, and a beautiful wood mantel with inlaid votive candles wraps around the wall.

Loree Rodkin > Diamonds Are a Girl's Best Friend

For a tiny woman, Loree Rodkin lives large. Actually, by any standards, she's one of Los Angeles' biggest presences. All roads in this town often lead to her, as her influence is felt from circle to circle, entertainment biz to fashion to music. Large is the adjective that best describes the often irreverent diamond jewelry she designs for rock stars and rabid fans across the globe and for her tumbling mane of dark hair that almost overwhelms her small frame. "Large" does not even begin to convey her social span, which reaches from Los Angeles to New York to St. Tropez to Mykonos to Miami to Tokyo and now to Moscow; her travel lust, which frequently leads her to all those places; and her imagination and its very visual manifestation—seen, yes, largely, in her highly original style of dress.

"Maximalism" is a word that could describe her life. Before designing jewelry, she managed some of Hollywood's most visible actors and, before that, designed houses for other famous folk. Rodkin's last Hollywood Hills home was a temple of maximalism: filled to the brim with Gothic crosses, dark fringed lamps, heavy velvets, and religious artifacts from churches. (One of her jewelry collections is appropriately called "Loree Rodkin Gothic," and her signature Gothic look had an enormous influence on her old friend Cher,

whose "Sanctuary" catalog of Gothic furniture Loree helped create.)

Then one day, a few years ago, she looked around at the foreboding environment and said, "No more. I'm done." Just like that.

Explains Rodkin, "After spending so much time in Bali and Japan —the Park Hyatt in Tokyo, where they shot *Lost in Translation,* was a real intoxicant for me—the serenity of my surroundings made me feel, when I came home to my flea-market obsession for objects, that my eyes were bleeding. So I bought this house in 2002 and in four months turned it into a pristine sanctuary—highly stylized in a minimal way with very warm lighting. I had to surrender my longtime obsession with objects and pare it down."

Now the only noticeable "objects" are large Buddha heads— the enormous scale of which added the quiet drama Rodkin was going for. "I set design rather than decorate," she says. "I have no formal training—it's not like I went to school for this. But to me, it's all under the heading of 'visual.' I consulted a contractor, who told me what I could and couldn't do with the house, but I was my own designer. To me, an architect would just get in the way. I sketched all the furniture myself, then worked with an upholsterer, bringing him swatches of fabric I loved: a chenille I had loomed for the sofas, an iridescent leather for the dining-room chairs, and stingray for the end tables. I had the fabrics woven to go with my palette. I kept stuffing and restuffing chairs and sofas —I mean, like six times, till I was happy. I kept wanting different heights and different degrees of hardness and softness. I covered my dining-room chairs with marshmallow leather (don't call it white!) and finished the skirts, so they would look like dresses."

Rodkin chose a wash of textures and light. "Lighting is the art in a room as far as I'm concerned. Light sources should never just be lamps. They need to be illuminated objects, and everything—I mean everything—should be on a rheostat [lighting intensity controlled by a dimming switch]. I just put light where I wanted to see a glow. All of the unusual lamps are from objects—very few began life as lamps."

The outdoor pool and Zen garden were, once again, pretty much landscaped by her. "I hired a landscaper to take me to a nursery," she says, "but then I told her every single plant to buy. She had no idea how to create a Zen garden."

The feeling now, indoor and out, is more quiet storm than rock 'n' roll temple. The large living room fireplace was fashioned in sand. "Fire and fireplaces are living theater—sensual, peaceful. Flames through sand gave me the linear drama I wanted." The twinkle of city lights from a view over West Hollywood and Century City appeals to Rodkin more than a vista of mountains: "I'm a city girl all the way."

This area, often referred to as "the Bird area" or "the Doheny Hills," is perfect for Angelenos who like the feeling of rustic life but are in fact minutes from a soy latte and a hot hotel. "This is my fourth house in this neighborhood," Rodkin laughs. "I may have design ADD, but when it comes to neighborhood, I'm a creature of habit. It's probably the only constant in my life: my neighborhood. And my shoe collection. I'm a homing pigeon for the Bird streets."

To understand just how antithetical this house is to her colorful life, you have to catch up on some Loree lore: she comes from the hybrid world of Hollywood and rock 'n' roll counterculture, owing to an eclectic career that's spanned, among other things and people, designing houses for Rod Stewart, Olivia Newton John, Alice Cooper, Don Henley, and Bernie Taupin—in a maximalistic collecting frenzy that began with art nouveau and climaxed with her signature Gothic look.

Then there's Loree's historic love life, once chronicled in *Vanity*

Fair. "I used to be as well known for my boyfriends as my career," she laughs, having grown bored with the notion herself. "I didn't know I was being nervy by going out with all these major guys. I was just too ignorant—a little girl from Chicago who got to L.A. at nineteen—to know any better."

Her brief stint with naiveté didn't last long—nor has much else in her life, as she's moving too fast for anything, for anyone, or for any trend, to keep up. "Yes, I've got ADD when it comes to design, and pretty much everything else," she admits. "It's just about stimulation—or lack thereof. I have to keep moving and morphing. I can sleep when I'm dead. Nike says it best: 'Life is short. Play hard.'"

After doing the king of Kuwait's nephew's homes in Los Angeles and New York on an exalted unlimited budget, she says, "I just couldn't go back to fabric swatches. There was nowhere to go but down." So she switched course and started managing the dancer Alexander Godunov. "He didn't know anyone, and I was the most connected person he'd ever met. I didn't know anything about ballet, but I just thought, What the hell? I can only fail." Instead, in unique Rodkin fashion, she paved her own course and never had a second of the kind of conventional fear that clings to most people. Judd Nelson, John Malkovich, Kyra Sedgwick, Brad Pitt, Robert Downey Jr., and Sarah Jessica Parker became part of a stable of supercool young actors she guided to a different kind of Hollywood stardom: edgier.

When the madness of Downey's well-documented drug problems kept her up at night, Rodkin—who'd demanded to self-design her mother's annual Christmas presents of jewelry from age twelve— started sketching jewelry designs to stay busy. "I met a couple who repaired Cartier jewelry and they let me play with vintage stones— really teaching me to make jewelry. Nobody was into vintage jewelry in the late eighties—which is hard to believe now. I started wearing my own stuff, and Maxfield's asked to carry it in 1989." She stumbled into jewelry design like she'd stumbled into managing actors, then took to it with the ferocity she brings to everything else.

While Rodkin kept a few clients till 1994, she began to get her jewelry—diamonds fashioned into Maltese crosses, Gothic religious symbols, and other bigger and edgier shapes than diamonds had been used in before—into stores like Stanley Korshak and Hirshleifer's. First, the rock stars came running for rings and bulky bracelets: Ringo Starr, Yoko Ono, Steven Tyler of Aerosmith,

Rodkin, who sells her recognizable rock 'n' roll jewelry all over the world, recently expanded the line to include leather bags and sunglasses. When not working out of her studio, she can create in her tranquil home office, drawing inspiration from a curved leather loveseat and oversized photos printed on canvas by Brian English, a former assistant to Herb Ritts.

Lionel Richie, Bruce Springsteen and Patti Scialfa, Cher, Courtney Love. But it was Tyler and Cher who parachuted her onto the map. Then Hollywood came calling: Melanie Griffith, Kate Capshaw, Rita Wilson. And it sure didn't hurt that there wasn't anyone cool or famous that Loree Rodkin hadn't met—or who hadn't heard of her. It was also the first fashioning of diamonds and precious stones that looked good with black leather. Sure, it was shiny happy jewelry—but with a dark, dramatic edge. It didn't look ostentatious, it looked . . . dangerous.

Like every other career move by Rodkin, the step of going into the jewelry design business was bold—and success was immediate. In the United States, Loree Rodkin jewelry is now sold in more than fifty stores, including Neiman Marcus, and in freestanding Loree Rodkin boutiques in Japan and thirty-eight Loree departments in Japanese department stores. There are also scents, candles, incense, and bags. And the jewelry has not grown less intimidating but *more* so. One three-part joint ring seems to have been designed to give observers the so-called middle finger in full-bling oversized style. A boldfaced diamond

ring reads FUCK YOU. Rodkin herself rarely goes out without these now-classic rock iconoclast accessories or without giant diamond pendants in the shapes of evil eyes, daggers, weapons, and crosses. "Which has got nothing to do with religion," she laughs. "And everything to do with belief, passion, art—and extremes."

This brings us back to her house: an extreme of sand-toned Balinese Zen modernism, in complete—and maximal—contrast to her last house, which famously held elaborate velvet fringed lamps, church pews, animal skins, Flintstone furniture, stained-glass windows, and Oriental rugs—not to mention giant crosses and elaborate religious art.

"If I had to describe my nesting sense right now, I'd say it's absence of chaos. It all changed after I started spending time in Bali. I need a really quiet and peaceful environment now. What I do for a living is filled with minute detail. I look at my house as minute minimalism. I'm the oxymoron of minimalism."

Which once again comes down to the essential Rodkin theme: stimulation. "I need every corner of my vista to please me—and amuse me. I just can't bear to be bored. Not for one minute."

High atop the Hollywood Hills with views that stretch to the ocean sits Rodkin's bronze Buddha head, imported from Bali.

"The feeling, indoor and out,
is more quiet storm than
rock 'n' roll temple."

The ornate teak Buddha welcomes
visitors as they drive into Rodkin's
Balinese oasis. The lush landscaping
is horsetail and vinca, with potted
flax plants.

In the backyard, hand-carved female deities adorn an imported Balinese pavilion. Rodkin added an Indian-style bed found in L.A. for lazy days spent lounging by the pool.

The dining room has a Zen feel, with a nineteenth-century Victorian oak dining-room table and iridescent marshmallow leather chairs designed by Rodkin.

Rodkin's use of natural materials, like the sleek blue Gascon limestone floor, rocks, and stone benches, gives one the feeling of "living outside."

Rodkin's impeccable taste and experience as an interior designer for friends such as Rod Stewart are apparent in the flawless decor of her home. All of the furniture covered in skins—like the soft crème leather sofa—was designed by Rodkin herself and custom-made in Los Angeles.

One of the gilded Victorian turn-of-the-century columns sits in the long curved hallway with an eighteenth-century mirror on the other end.

The oversized master bath, with soaking tub, steam shower, and extra vanity space, is made of riff-cut oak. This is where Rodkin "usually contemplates what to wear that night." A chaise of her own design, covered in a rich caramel chenille that matches her bedroom walls, sits on a cowhide rug.

Renowned costume designer Susan Becker and her husband, movie director Harold Becker, live in the house that everyone dreams of having. It is truly their refuge. "One feels at home the minute you walk in the house. You can't help it," says Susan. Although the couple has been looking for another home for twenty years, Susan admits that the true reason they haven't found one is because "the idea of leaving this one is simply unbearable." She has told interested friends, "The very minute we decide to sell the house, you will be the first to know," but Becker feels like the idea of visiting the buyer in her former beloved home would be "just so devastating," so those friends look to be in for a long wait for that call.

Having moved to Southern California exclusively for their work, Susan says that the couple will always feel somewhat like transplants in Los Angeles. It is their house that grounds them here. Susan and Harold are from the East Coast—she Philadelphia and he New York—and living in Los Angeles somehow always meant living in a Spanish house to them. "There is no other place besides Mexico or a Spanish-influenced country where you can find a house like this. It has a historical feeling about it that just feels right for this city." Though they did look at houses by famed L.A. architects Richard Neutra and Rudolf M. Schindler, something about this big Spanish house with its magnificence and history just drew them in.

Built in 1928 and located in the historic Outpost Drive area of the Hollywood Hills, the house was purchased by the Beckers while Harold was directing friend Tom Cruise in *Taps* (circa 1980). Susan, a self-professed "career girl," says she really only remembers dates by what films she or her husband were working on at the time. Remarkably, the Beckers are only the second owners of the house. The first owners built the house and had children, grandchildren, and great-grandchildren here.

In the center of the house is a spectacular atrium filled with lush exotic plants and Susan's extensive and prized collection of Bauer, Teco, and Weller pottery. The atrium had a tremendous influence on the couple's decision to buy the house. Susan says, "My husband walked in and fell in love with the atrium. It is pure romance." Equipped with a retractable glass roof, it is the epitome of Southern California indoor/outdoor living, providing an amazing setting for dining al fresco—even when it rains. "You can live in a way in Los Angeles that you can't live in New York City. It just doesn't exist," says Susan. "The atrium is the heart of the house," adds Harold. "Our New York apartment had a similar conservatory —but obviously on a smaller scale."

As if the stunning atrium were not enough, the house has a magnificent garden that has been featured on the illustrious L.A. Garden Tour. Because the garden was one of the reasons they fell in love with the house, they have felt a tremendous responsibility and loyalty to keeping it up. It was also very important to the Beckers to keep the aesthetic of the outdoor space consistent with the fundamental themes of the house. So, instead of making it easier for herself by "laying down some grass," as her real estate developer father suggested, Susan kept with the original scheme of the gardens. Lovingly tended by their longtime gardener, Refugio, the grounds are replete with indigenous plants and trees, with some additions made by Susan along the way— pampas grasses, lavender, olive trees, a rose garden, and a fantastic garden of giant sculptured cacti. "Life here in the suburbs of L.A. does have a few pluses," says Harold. "The gardens, warm weather . . . and of course 'the Business.'"

Susan did the interior decor herself and admits that there really was no big conscious effort in putting it all together. What is evident throughout the space, however, is the distinct style that is so present in both of their professional lives. Susan has been involved in fashion and costume design all her life and has worked on films as diverse as *True Romance, Sgt. Bilko,* and *Days of Thunder.* She designed her own line of clothing for a time and is currently making a dress for good friend Madonna. Though Susan has more of an eclectic style than her husband—she loves large Mexican piñatas, Le Corbusier, and the perfect white cotton shirt —she says that her tastes are also simple and classic. Known as one of Los Angeles' most fashionable and original women, Susan loves timeless clothes. Some of her favorites include Hermès, gowns by Oscar de la Renta, a Chanel suit or jacket, and a great pair of Levi's.

Harold, an old-school purist, is as detailed in his work as a photographer and film director (his directorial work includes *Vision Quest, Sea of Love, The Onion Field,* and *Malice*) as he is in his personal style—wearing only black, gray, or navy. "I came to L.A. because as a director, the work is here. Although films are rarely shot here in their entirety, the business is mainly here. We could live in New York City, but . . . a pool in the middle of Manhattan?

a giant magnolia tree outside on Fifth Avenue? No . . . we like the peace and quiet up in these hills . . . It's good for thinking."

Susan and Harold bought most of the furniture on their travels. Susan admits that they have been lugging much of it around for years. They bought the old wood table in their kitchen several years ago in England. They've had the Mies van der Rohe chairs for many years—so long that Susan doesn't remember where she got them. Everything in the house has a history. She obtained a lot of the pottery in her collection, including the Catalina dishes she uses every day, at swap meets around the world. Both of the Beckers are great fans of the Bauhaus school of design and architect Frank Lloyd Wright. "I have long been an educated fan of architecture," says Harold. "Susan and I built one of the great houses—designed by Norman Jaffe—in the Hamptons. But it was the romance of this 1920s Spanish house that attracted us."

The Beckers have used everything in their house with such great affection that the idea of getting rid of something and buying new seems almost foreign. When the fabric on the cushions wears out, Susan makes new ones. When the chairs in the atrium (bought in a Paris flea market) started to change from their natural color from years of wear, Susan had them painted green. Harold has designed some of the chairs in the house as well. Every once in a while Susan does think that she will get a new dining room table but never quite gets around to it. She recently bought herself a Charles Eames white leather office chair but she now thinks she will most likely get the old one in her office repaired and put the new one somewhere else in the house.

"It was never our intention to bring anything into the home that didn't fit us or the house. We have tried to keep it original," Susan says. She loves the light that comes through her house in the afternoons and believes that no truly great house in Los Angeles should be without a fantastic espresso machine, great lighting, great seating, and a great bed—with some Pratesi sheets, of course.

Previous page: Susan, in a silver Marni pantsuit, is considered one of L.A.'s most fashionable women. She also designs clothes and is currently working on a dress for Madonna. Harold is the quintessential Renaissance man: years ago he designed department store windows, was a major still photographer in New York, and designed several pieces of furniture in their existing home.

The focal point of the house is the spectacular glass-topped atrium, filled with exotic plants, which requires a special ventilating fan system. A gardener comes three times a week to tend the atrium and property. The large pots are Bauer from the 1930s and '40s, and the green pottery on the table is valuable Teco, designed by Frank Lloyd Wright. The roof retracts for Susan's famous dinner parties "under the stars."

The Beckers have added to the extensive wild garden, which has been featured on the annual L.A. Garden Tour, since buying the house in the early 1980s. On the left is a tree that Tom Cruise gave the Beckers as a Christmas gift fifteen years ago. It is now over thirty feet tall. Refugio, their beloved gardener, has been tending the grounds for years.

The living room has a real old Hollywood feel, with a red velvet couch and two black leather chairs, all designed by Harold. The Persian rug was found in London and the small black leather and lacquered wood chair in the corner is an Eileen Gray Transit chair. A vintage Walker Evans photograph hangs above the Texas limestone fireplace.

"It was the romance of this 1920s Spanish house that attracted us."

The chic yet simple dining room contains a black lacquer Mies van der Rohe table and chairs, topped with a green glass decanter by Retro. The beautiful oak wood floors are original to the house. Susan loves to hunt for the large dolls—which are Mexican piñatas—at small shops in downtown Los Angeles.

Susan and Harold added the Mexican stone lap pool, which overlooks the garden, after they purchased the house.

The large planters are from clay pottery maker Gladding McBean, which has been around since 1875, and the funky Chinese "opium bed" is covered in gorgeous Fortuny fabric.

Susan decorated the home after they moved in and has left it for the most part unchanged. A large Fortuny "movie" lamp, the vintage Bill Brandt photograph behind her, and stacks of books add Hollywood flair to this corner of the living room.

Harold used this antique large-format camera during his days as a still photographer. The Mies van der Rohe black leather chaise has been a staple in every Becker home, and on the back wall hang several vintage black and white prints by photography masters August Sander and Andre Kertesz.

Harold's bulldog, Shug, is a frequent companion on strolls through the Beckers' famed garden.

As owner of the chicest vintage shop in Los Angeles, Decades, Cameron Silver not only put vintage clothes onto Hollywood's high-fashion map, he also put vintage into the stars' closets. He's dressed Nicole Kidman, Reneé Zellweger, Winona Ryder, Diane Lane, Cameron Diaz, and other famous women in vintage high couture for awards shows, almost single-handedly bringing names like Loris Azzaro, Emilio Pucci, Koos Van den Akker, Ossie Clark, and Pauline Trigère back into fashion vogue. He's also responsible for making slightly tatty Hermès Birkin and Kelly bags more de rigueur than new ones. In short, Silver taught modern Hollywood how to appreciate the older gems in its closets. In a town with a deep-seated prejudice against any kind of aging, that's no small feat. He definitely brought old Hollywood glamour to new Hollywood, which in turn brought him worldwide fashion attention.

Very much a Beverly Hills boy, Silver was not one of those ordinary Hollywood kids: he loved movies, true; but he also loved fashion, history, and culture of all kinds. He set his sights on a career in singing—in particular, German cabaret. Unlike most kids raised in Los Angeles, he didn't want to be the next John Travolta or Richard Gere—more the next Bertolt Brecht. Or, perhaps more realistically, Kurt Weill.

Well, that didn't ultimately prove realistic at all. But it did prove that Silver was a cultured, worldly guy, focused on the rare and unusual—and not exactly what is in current favor. When it came time for him and longtime partner, interior designer and actor Jeff Snyder, to lay down roots in 1999, the so-called Elliot House, built by Viennese architect R. M. Schindler, was a more than appropriate fit: appointed with all kinds of original Schindlerisms in the foothills of Los Feliz, the architecturally pure and proud house built on a steep uphill slope had seen, well, better days. So Silver and Snyder worked their magic with the architectural team of Leo Marmol and Ron Radziner, taking a rough found jewel and polishing it into a vintage trilevel gem.

"It was the third house we saw on day one," said Jeff, "and we knew we loved it—but it was in all kinds of structural disarray."

"I knew it was the right house when I saw the garage going up and into the hill," adds Silver. "It's so architecturally significant—and it was a hint of what's to come. I knew it was the right house even before we made it inside. I just said, 'This is it.'"

Constructed in 1930, the house was built as two stories by Schindler for Robert Elliot, his insurance agent. Nine years later, the architect returned and added the third and lowest level of the house, where the master bedroom is now located. When Silver and Snyder saw it, subsequent owners had painted much of the original wood white and had actually ripped out an original built-in Schindler desk in the living room. Silver and Snyder set out to reconstruct it according to the original plans and restore its architectural purity, with some modifications.

Silver and Snyder chose the firm of Marmol Radziner (which also restored Neutra's Kaufman House, the Gamble House in Pasadena, and Albert Frey's Loewy House) to conduct the renovations. They replaced much of the original plywood—Schindler made a point of using common materials everyone could afford—and reproduced Schindler's original forms, including a wonderful little kitchen window, ever so small enough to seem unimportant but magical enough to let a beam of light bleed onto the countertop and completely change the mood of the small kitchen. They replaced the original oakwood kitchen floor with fir, and put in three new windows.

"Marmol Radziner did seamless interpretations of Schindler's built-ins, which they saw in some of his other houses," says Snyder. "We had the couch in the living room built in." The result of their restoration won them all a 2005 Conservancy Award and a spot on the architectural tours of Los Angeles. "It's amazing," sighs Silver, "when you think it was close to bulldoze material when we bought it."

Silver and Snyder also decided to retain small side lights that illuminate both indoors and out. They make the house even more dramatic at night.

Schindler, who came from Austria to Chicago, relished the indoor/outdoor life of Southern California, and was a fan of indoor outdoor fireplaces, as is Snyder. "We wanted a gas fireplace, but then your only typical option is fake logs," Snyder explained. "So we did the fireplace with lava rocks." The effect, summer or winter, is both as dramatic as fire . . . and as serene as nature. And it floods the house with warmth.

The house manages to be uniquely modern, masculine, and reflective of some of the unique personality of its current owners. For instance, vintage Hermès ashtrays, desk supplies, and leather goods of all kinds grace almost every corner of the house.

"We all know about Cameron's Hermès obsession," sighs Jeff Snyder. Silver's Decades is known for its insider e-mail blasts to

Birkin and Kelly collectors announcing the arrival of vintage bags in myriad colors, sizes, and mints; they get snapped up on the Internet in virtual megabyte seconds. Turns out, though, that Silver does major snapping up himself. A quick tour of his large laundry room and master bedroom (on the house's bottom level in the side of the hill) reveals over forty vintage Hermès travel bags, in matte sueded alligator and all varieties of rare skin combos. Some of them even came from Catherine Deneuve's private Parisian collection. "Some of them are worth twelve thousand dollars," says Silver, hauling them out in his laundry room, an incongruous setting for this treasure bounty if there ever was one. "And some of them are worth forty thousand. What can I say? I'm just a freak for skins."

Most of the freestanding furniture this pair hunted came, of course, from a Paris flea market. A few stunning exceptions are a metal chair in the living room with a distressed leather seat and a 1960s bright brass swinging (literally) lamp procured at the Centre Pompidou. In the media room on the house's second level down, there's a reproduction of a Jean Prouve sitting chair from the 1930s, and a large MY SIN—LANVIN sign Silver found at the Rosebowl flea market. When Alber Elbaz, Lanvin's current design head, came to the house for a party to celebrate a Lanvin event at Barneys Beverly Hills, he wanted to buy it straight out from under them!

Another interesting element of the so-called TV room is a group of collages on the wall by an artist named Jarred Cairns. Turns out, he'd worked at Decades, and it all started when he sent Silver a collage postcard from a trip to Texas. "I said, Jarred, those collages are so interesting you should make larger pieces. Look at this one—he did this for my birthday one year," Silver says, pointing to what resembles a two-dimensional Joseph Cornell.

The outdoor furniture—on two sides of the house—is almost as interesting. A high deck on the top level, which formerly held a wood and stucco trellis covered with wisteria ("We had to take it off to paint and realized it hid some of the architectural details of the house") features a set of original 1930s Van Keppel Green string lounge chairs. It's the perfect spot from which Hank, their beloved dog, can covet the Haas avocados hanging on the nearby trees. "And he does eat most of them," says Snyder. The other level's large garden includes old chairs in green and white, white lanterns,

The large front windows off of the living room are Silver and Snyder's favorite feature of the house. "Something so simple and dramatic at the same time," says Snyder, "and they open up an entire wall of the house."

A 1980 view of the house by genius architectural photographer Julius Shulman, before Silver and Snyder shrouded the property in tall trees.

a couple of requisite Buddhas (no L.A. house is complete without them), and the other requisite item—the master grill.

The guest bedroom is a world of its own: it veers off into the eccentric, with Hermès accessories everywhere, William Claxton photos of his wife, 1960s icon Peggy Moffat (the couples are friends), and a fluffy white fur blanket on all-white bedding. The houses' entire book collection—and it's a big one—lines the shelves in the bedroom.

The master bathroom has a stone bathtub, a concrete floor, and a shower with shells lining it. "Very masculine," laughs Silver. But it actually is—if you don't count the shells. Also housed nearby in the master bedroom is Cameron's collection of vintage caftans. An always impeccably turned-out gent, it's hard to imagine him actually wearing them, though; his normal clothes are tailored to a tee. "It's only when we have parties," says Jeff, "and he can come upstairs and make a huge entrance!"

"Here's the best one I've ever seen," says Cameron, showing it off. "It's from the collection of a ballet dancer, and he and his wife were huge collectors of exotic textiles. This is so chic, I told Vanessa Seward (the head designer for Loris Azzaro) that Azzaro should do these." It's easy to see why the French fashion house made Silver a consultant a few years ago.

So not all is totally "masculine" under this roof—but who's to say what that word really means anymore these days? "The house is what we wanted it to be," says Jeff. "Warm, earthy, masculine, and modern. But I don't think modern has to be cold. Modern does not have to be sterile."

Clearly not.

Previous page: Hank shares a rare moment of downtime with his owners. The architecture firm and Modernist restoration wizards Marmol Radziner led the renovation of the Schindler house in Los Feliz and custom-made many of the furnishings, such as the green silk chenille sofa in the living room. Silver sits in a vintage chair by Frank Lloyd Wright from Wright's Wynn House in Wisconsin, and Snyder stands in front of a painting by local artist Kim Fisher. The stainless-steel dining room table with marble top was custom-made by Blake Simpson.

"The house is what we wanted it to be—warm, earthy, masculine, and modern."

The original glass doors designed by Schindler needed only slight renovation when Silver and Snyder bought the house, which was built for the architect's insurance agent. Silver and Snyder discovered the hanging lamp in a flea market in Paris and the desk chair seen at left was originally designed for the Centre Pompidou.

The living room shows off the clean and simple lines that Schindler made famous. The fireplace was originally open to the outside; Silver and Snyder enclosed it "to keep little animals out." They also added gas and lava stones. L.A. designer Blake Simpson custom-made the low coffee table for the house. The floors in the living room were completely redone in sleek fir wood.

A vintage Gucci lamp, gold Hermès clock, and picture frames line the simple built-in desk in the living room, which was fabricated based on Schindler's original design.

It was important to Silver, Snyder, and Marmol Radziner to preserve the original corrugated metal and wood ceiling in the library, a recognizable Schindler feature. Marmol Radziner custom-made the couch and ottomans, above which hangs a painting by L.A. artist and friend Jarred Cairns. Silver and Snyder treasure the small George Nelson table, circa 1948, under the window. Silver, whose store Decades deals in the decidedly coveted clothes of Lanvin by Alber Elbaz, found the perfect MY SIN—LANVIN sign (visible beneath the window) at the legendary Rosebowl flea market.

A replica of the original plant box sits at the top of the staircase, and the wood wall design that Schindler built to enable light to flow into the kitchen was also re-created.

When Silver and Snyder purchased the house in 1999 the "kitchen had been done over in Ikea." Marmol Radziner redesigned the space to reflect the original kitchen, with the cutouts that allow the sun in. Translucent glass bottles found in a Paris flea market—which were originally used in a French perfume factory—are suffused in sunlight on the top shelf.

Silver and Snyder kick back on their deck. Japanese maple trees, giant bamboo, and tall grass completely shroud the property, and help maintain privacy given that the house has no window coverings. The outdoor chairs and ottoman—strung with rope—are by Van Keppel Green and the ceramic pots planted with Irish moss come from Architectural Pottery in L.A.

The only part of the Schindler house that is visible from the street is the steel-reinforced garage and the structure above it, which was originally meant to be a wisteria-covered trellis. Guests climb stairs surrounded by bamboo to reach the second level and entrance to the home.

Sun filters through the trees outside the guest bedroom of the Elliot House, built in 1930. A cantilevered window opens over the bed, and a reproduced Schindler Sling chair (at right) offers relaxation. William Claxton took the iconic black and white photograph of his wife, Peggy Moffat, during her days as a model. Silver's passion for Hermès is evident in the rich sheared mink throw on the bed and chic leather mat on the floor, both from the venerable French retailer.

Ask Hutton Wilkinson any question and the answer will involve a good story. A very good story. It could be about a piece of furniture, his house on Outpost Road, his multigenerational Angeleno upbringing, a piece of the Tony Duquette jewelry he designs for Bergdorf Goodman, Stanley Korshak in Chicago, or Geary's in Beverly Hills, or even how the longtime designer, decorator, and L.A. Renaissance man would possibly define himself.

"As a mistake!" is his lightning-like answer, but like everything else in his life, nothing could be further from the truth—or nearer to the truth. For him, as with most highly evolved individuals, truth is subjective. "Things have always come to me," he muses. "I don't know why." Maybe because of his highly adventurous soul.

Mistake or not, Wilkinson's been a well-known decorator and designer in Los Angeles for thirty years, and both his father and his grandfather were well-known L.A. architects. Tracing the genealogy of people and objects is another of his passions.

"My great-granddaddy was the first city attorney of Los Angeles—who was one of the five founders of the city of Pasadena," he says. "One of his daughters, Eugenia Floride Hutton, married Mansfield Wilkinson, my grandfather. In 1918, my grandfather started building movie studios (one of which is the current Raleigh Studios), dressing rooms for W. C. Fields and Mae West, and houses. My father was one of the first graduates of Beverly Hills High School, Marshall Phillip Wilkinson."

As an adult, his father joined his grandfather in the family firm, and Hutton, prodigy that he was out of six children, virtually grew up in their architectural office. "They called me 'the little architect,'" he laughs. He'd leave the family home in Hancock Park every day and either go to the office or a building site. So he of course gravitated toward architecture—until he saw *Camelot* in high school and decided to be a costume designer. "But then I craved attention," he says, "so I decided to become a decorator. Besides, decorators were the ones riding around in Rolls-Royces in those days."

While attending Fairfax High in Hollywood, he met his future wife, Ruthie, and they married in 1976. Around this time he also began taking art classes. There, a teacher turned his world upside down by introducing him to the work of Tony Duquette: decorator, costume designer, set designer extraordinaire, who'd created homes for J. Paul Getty and the Duchess of Windsor, costumes for Broadway, sets for many film musicals, and anything else he could get his hands on. "My teacher taught me all about Chippendale, Regency, and Louis XIV and XV furniture—but best of all, she showed me Tony Duquette's scrapbooks. They were among the most beautiful things I'd ever seen." At Woodbury

College, while Hutton was studying to be a decorator, a teacher told him the maestro Duquette was looking for volunteers.

"Next thing I knew, I'd quit school, and went to work for Tony for free for two years," Wilkinson recounts with a smile. "I lived at home; I was eighteen. Tony was staging an exhibition at the Municipal Gallery at Barnsdale Park and he had 150 volunteers to help set it up —and it was beautiful—but the next day, I was the only one who showed up to clean up. That's when Tony knew I was serious."

After that, Hutton worked for Tony full time for the next three years, for the grand sum of fifty dollars every two weeks. After this five-year tenure, Hutton left and opened his own decorating business, quickly gathering clients—from whom he learned that real estate was where the real money was. "So I took some money and Tony and I became real estate developers together." As Duquette grew older, Wilkinson often took on his decorating jobs. "He was such a mentor to me," says Hutton. "I mean, he introduced me to Claudette Colbert, George Cukor, Vincente Minnelli, Loretta Young, and Mary Martin. One day I was in Tony's home, Dawnridge, and I saw Merle Oberon descending the stairs. I got to know Mary Pickford and Garbo, Dolores del Rio, Rosalind Russell, and Fred Astaire through Tony."

And all of this predates the now-famous Duquette jewelry collection by years. Tony had been collecting raw stones for some time, and he made some exotic handmade jewelry for his wife, Elizabeth (commonly known as "Beegle,"), a painter, and for a few private collectors across the globe. In the early 1990s, Tony and Hutton took a trip around the world, and when they got to India, Tony decided to buy a lot of gems—two suitcases full of citrines, emeralds, and so forth—which Hutton had to carry.

When they arrived in Bali, Hutton said, "I told him I would not walk one step further with those suitcases. So we sat on the beach and taped them together into two hundred necklaces, then found someone to cast them. We promptly brought them back to L.A.—and never tried to sell them."

In 1996, Dawn Mello at Bergdorf Goodman in New York got wind of the ornate necklaces and invited Hutton and Tony to make eighteen-karat gold, diamond, ruby, and emerald necklaces exclusively for the store. The Duquette collection immediately took off and was seen on the necks, ears, and fingers of Oscar nominees and stars such as Duquette's neighbor Sharon Stone. Hutton has kept it going, even after Tony's death at age eighty-five in 1999,

and his pictures often show up in the pages of W and Vogue.

Not only is Hutton Wilkinson a man of many stories, he is also a man of many houses. After developing real estate with Duquette for years—buying apartment buildings and redoing them—Hutton purchased Duquette's home in Benedict Canyon (the famous Dawnridge) and his Malibu estate. He continues to use them as visual inspiration and as studios where he creates the jewelry. (They're also the site of many an exotic fashion shoot for major magazines like Italian Vogue and the New York Times Magazine.) But he has been steadfast to the home featured here, which he purchased for Ruthie and himself twenty years ago through the oddest coincidence—one that seems more like synchronicity, really.

"Ruthie and I were driving along Outpost Road and saw a FOR SALE sign—on a house my father and grandfather had built together. Turned out, it was untouched since 1936—the last owners had let it sit there empty and didn't sell for thirty years! I took Tony to see it and it was much too square for him. But Ruthie wanted that house. And my father sent me his original plans for it, so I could restore it."

During renovation they pulled up the carpet—only to find polished hardwood floors. The eggshell paint from 1936 doesn't chip —so Wilkinson simply glazed over it. "Everything in the home is original," he says, three fireplaces included. "The house had never even had a television in it." In twenty years, the Wilkinsons have redecorated the residence three times—most recently in 2005. "It's now more of a modern version of an English thirties country house, inspired by the work of Elsie de Wolfe." (Wilkinson is the president of the Elsie de Wolfe Foundation—he succeeded Duquette in the role.) "It was also originally inspired by the Venetian paintings all over the house that Tony gave me—they are from the collection of the late-seventeenth-century Baroness d'Erlanger, who bought them from the Morosini family in Venice, of the Palazzo Morosini. She came to America and opened one of Los Angeles' first gay bars, Gala, where Spago used to be on Sunset. Everybody went there, gay or straight, in the 1940s. Somehow the paintings wound up in Tony's possession."

The swimming pool was built to resemble a Venetian canal— Wilkinson admits a major infatuation with the northern Italian antic city. "I'm on the board of Save Venice," he quips, "and I have been known to have waiters serve food at parties wearing serving gondolas, front and back."

Many of the other flamboyant or ornate pieces in the house

The pasha in his castle: Wilkinson reclines in the library on a sofa covered in a vicuna throw from Bolivia (above which hangs a painting of a Russian princess formerly in the collection of the Baroness d' Erlanger). A sleek custom-made cocktail table with an antique Coromandel lacquered panel top stands out in the English deal-paneled room.

came to him organically via movie sets and back lots. "MGM once called up Tony and myself and said, 'Come over to the lot, we're giving away a lot of stuff.' Well, I got a pavilion for my garden, eighteenth-century French fireplaces, the doors of Tara from *Gone With the Wind*, Roman gates—it was endless."

Duquette gave him as wedding gifts the green brocade fabric from Scalamandré, which they used as curtains, and the obelisks that stand by the pool. The ceiling in the dining room is Pompeian red, to go with the Coromandel screens that emulate the design sense of Coco Chanel. "The breakfast room is all made out of Indian bedspreads," laughs Hutton. "And Ruthie got a dress made out of one of them. We call it her Camouflage Dress."

The word *whimsy* is almost too obvious a choice to describe the world of the Outpost house, which is clearly influenced by

Duquette's Dawnridge decor of utter and complete individuality, luxurious materials, and found Dada materials like seashells (which cover the Dawnridge living-room walls) or skateboards lining a porch. "I call it the Tao of Decoration," says Hutton. "You follow the path of least resistance! I don't buy furniture. I never actually have. It just . . . appears. It always has. I really couldn't tell you where most of this stuff comes from."

Previous page: Coral teakwood palace screens carved in the traditional Chinese snowflake pattern frame the fireplace in the main living room. The Baroness d' Erlanger acquired and brought to Los Angeles the seventeenth-century Venetian painting that originally hung in the Palazzo Morosini and now graces the Wilkinsons' wall. Also from Venice are the lacquered eighteenth-century chairs. Wilkinson had a hand in all of the fine design details, like the Venetian coral branches mounted in eighteenth-century gilded wooden urns that sit on the mantel.

"I call it the Tao of Decoration . . .
You follow the path of least
resistance!"

Opulence is the word in the English deal-paneled library. Framed family photos sit on a steel and bronze desk by Jansen, below seventeenth-century Coromandel panels attached to the wall. Wilkinson imported the aubergine taffeta draperies and printed cotton pelmets from India. The ceiling is painted Pompeian red.

A stunning Tony Duquette chandelier from the 1960s glitters in the ornate white pine–paneled dining room. Wilkinson found the carved silver chairs on a trip to Rajasthan. He calls the green nineteenth-century Chinese vases a mystery, "possibly made to look like jade for the Thai market." The framed prints on the wall depict a Chinese palace, Yuan Ming Yuan, which was designed for the Emperor Chen Lung in the seventeenth century. Lord Elgin, who led the joint British and French military forces, destroyed the palace after the Boxer Rebellion as punishment for the "wicked Chinese."

Modeled after the Wilkinsons' favorite city, the shimmering blue tile lap pool was built to look like a Venetian canal. Recently, they discovered the original landscaping plans from 1936, which revealed a planned rose garden where the ten-by-thirty-foot pool sits. Fans of the movie *Singin' in the Rain* might recognize the goats spitting water, which were used in several MGM movies. The blue and white antique Chinese porcelain ginger jars and jardinieres came from Thailand.

Wilkinson wears a pajama set he had made in New Delhi from old Indian saris because, as he says, "Ruth and I are the only two people in Los Angeles who are up all night long and go from pajamas to evening clothes on a regular basis."

A Georgian canopied bed, used in one of the *Thin Man* films, graces the master bedroom, beside which sits a nineteenth-century lacquered English tea table. Paintings by Julian La Trobe feature various rooms in houses where the Wilkinsons have lived. A precious and highly treasured First Empire Aubusson carpet adds to the room's quiet sophistication.

Famed decorator Elsie de Wolfe gave the eighteenth-century turquoise lacquered dressing table to Tony Duquette as a gift. Duquette then passed it on to Ruth for her first apartment. Later the Wilkinsons discovered several other pieces—the bed, some armchairs, and jewelry box—in the same color and began collecting all that they could find. The dressing table in their master bedroom holds various photographs in antique French frames, including that of Hutton's grandparents' 1910 wedding in Paris, Elizabeth Duquette at Pickfair in 1949, Hutton's mother in 1947, and Hutton and Ruth at Tony's studio in 1976.

You might run into anyone from George Clooney to Ed Ruscha at one of David's renowned parties. The property really is the ultimate bachelor pad, with a back patio and lawn that sweeps down to a pool with magnificent views.

Los Angeles is a city full of dreamers, and contrary to popular belief, some of them stay here to fulfill those dreams. Born in the city of "sun-baked people with half-baked ideas," David Codikow grew up in Los Angeles, but he now sees himself as "a citizen of the world." A lawyer in the music industry for fifteen years, he and his firm, Codikow, Carroll, Guido & Groffman, represented indie record labels, executives, and clients such as Marilyn Manson, Nirvana, Ben Harper, Dave Matthews, and Jay Z. Codikow is cofounder and co-owner of the wildly successful Vans Warped Tour, and he and his partner, Dana DuFine, manage the rock royalty group Velvet Revolver (made up of members from Guns N' Roses and fronted by Stone Temple Pilots' Scott Weiland).

With the constant traveling that comes with a rock 'n' roll life, you would think that travel is the last thing Codikow would want to do with his free time. Interestingly, what Codikow loves most about his house is the fact that it simultaneously centers him and takes him to the places around the world that he's visited. Objects brought back from Rome, Fez, Marrakech, and Berlin, to name a few, create a feeling of a wonderfully eclectic international bazaar that is neither understated nor overwhelming. It is quirky and elegant at the same time. It all just fits.

When Codikow sold his previous house in 1998, he told his broker to look for "the ugliest house with the best possible view in Beverly Hills," and the broker complied, finding him something that he likens to "Home Depot meets Caesar's Palace." Codikow planned to design the place himself, so all he needed was the view. He ended up choosing one high above the famed Sunset Strip. The house took about a year to design, with the help of architect Kevin Cozen, and about two and a half years to build. "I knew Kevin would be able to design and build exactly what I had envisioned," says Codikow. Its walls curve, making you feel embraced by the house the minute you sit down, and almost the entire backside of the house is glass, so every room affords a view of the city. Codikow had built the framework of his dreams; now he just needed to fill it.

Codikow wanted to handle the interior design himself and set out to create a space that would reflect his personality as much as the structure of the house did. This meant creating "something that was contemporary, yet had an extremely warm sensibility about it that you almost couldn't define." Most important, he wanted a place that immediately spoke of adventure and curiosity, so he planned to fill the house with things that he was curious or excited about—his books (he has more than three thousand), ideas (there is a considerable amount of Eastern-influenced furniture and decor), and the elements (the house, filled with wood and iron, allows him to watch the skies from its numerous windows and glass doors).

Intrigued by the warmth and light of the Mediterranean, Greece in particular, Codikow chose to saturate the house with deep reds and playful blues. He made a concerted effort to incorporate the light and color from this part of the world but has also tried to remain loyal to the house's own natural rhythms and elements. He wanted the glass, wood floors, and wrought iron to stand out, to evoke their own feelings. There is no place where this is more evident or speaks more clearly to Codikow's overall vision for the house than the all-glass suspension bridge connecting the living room and the dining room. "I wanted to walk on air," he says. Codikow is attracted to things "that compel and repel you" at the same time. The glass bridge forces you to feel both intrigued and scared simultaneously; "you have the curiosity to step on it, but you are almost afraid to at the same time," Codikow says. The bridge is a daily reminder that "there is always a feeling of adventure in the house."

A photography collector for over twenty years, Codikow also looks to images and artists for that sense of slightly dangerous adventure. His collection of over three hundred photographs reflects his wildly diverse yet distinct influences and taste. He loves the Surrealist movement that took place mostly in Czechoslovakia, Paris, and Berlin in the late 1920s and '30s, and he has a lot of the 1960s kitsch sexy glamour imagery by Wingate Paine, famous for his book *Mirror of Venus,* and Sam Haskins from his book *Cowboy Kate.* He mixes these with images from the Ballet Russes, which he bought for ten dollars at the Marché aux Puces in Paris; the fashion photography of Guy Bourdin and Irving Penn; and a photograph that a friend shot on the street. Other favorite artists include Jean Cocteau, Dora Maar (Picasso's muse), and Beatrice Wood (he owns a rare privately printed book on the artist, known as the "mother of Dada"). Above his staircase hangs what he calls "an iconic image" from the set of Michelangelo Antonioni's film *Blow-Up.* Found in a box in a flea market, the image shows famous 1960s Russian supermodel Veruschka being photographed. . . . No one really knows who took it. Codikow loves the idea that "a voyeur is obviously taking stills of a movie about voyeurism." He also finds the duality of feeling that he loves

so much in the work of German Surrealist Hans Bellmer. Bellmer's *La Poupée,* which Codikow has loaned to several museums, is one of his favorites. Bellmer photographed dolls that were falling apart, twisted, and tangled. The images are "both erotic and violent at the same time and were Bellmer's statement against Nazism and its idea of perfection," Codikow says.

Codikow looks at his house as "a piece of living art. . . . The house speaks creatively to me and I think that everyone's home should be a reflection of who they are as a person or who they want to be." He believes that "we travel to both find ourselves and lose ourselves" and the possessions in his own space reflect this idea. Heavily influenced by the music of different cultures—the beats and music indigenous to Africa, the flamenco music of Spain, and the iconic French music of Serge Gainsbourg, Codikow has tried to bring back a little of the feeling and mood from those places that the music evokes for him: "I think that I pick up different sensibilities from the sound, style, look and feel of the music and the performers which attract me to different areas of the world." Whether it is the mood of Paris' Left Bank, where poets, writers, and painters once lived and worked, or the bougainvillea, whitewashed walls, and concrete floors so evocative of Spanish flamenco culture that he has brought into the house, the music has helped Codikow "to define visual imagery through different cultural tones."

Codikow has traveled extensively to places like Capri, southern Spain, Morocco, and Paris to collect things to include in the house. Some of his discoveries arose from trips to his ranch in New Mexico or from the flea markets and swap meets he has scoured right here in Los Angeles. He has achieved his ultimate goal of being able to look around the house and dream of the places he's been—though the huge wooden front doors may be an exception, as they are originally from a jail in Peru. (Codikow found the fourteen-foot doors near Machu Picchu, had Native Americans bless and sage them, and had them shipped to Los Angeles.) Before moving in, however, he really didn't know where anything would go. He just knew that these pieces moved him, excited him, or intrigued him and that they would make his house what he wanted it to be. The very romantic double-sided clock from the metro in Paris, however, is a different story: the minute he saw it, he knew exactly where it would go. It is mounted on a wall in the center of the house, visible from almost every point, reminding him when the next train leaves and the new dream begins.

Codikow mixed contemporary elements with amazing found pieces in the design of his home, perched high in Beverly Hills. The huge wooden doors were originally from a jail in Peru and the doorbell is an old emergency call box found on a roadside in Los Angeles.

The master bedroom boasts Codikow's extensive book collection, which includes thousands of art, architecture, photography, travel, and design books, as well as over forty versions of *The Arabian Nights: Tales from a Thousand and One Nights.* Codikow found the leather chair seen in the background at the Pasadena Swap Meet many years ago.

Opposite: Codikow has a real flair for mixing quirky pieces from all over the world and making it look hip yet elegant. The birch tree wood table in the dining room was modeled after a similar piece from a Spanish castle in Grenada. It took a craftsman in Abiquiu, New Mexico, over a year to make. The chandelier came from an old ballroom in New Jersey, while the leather chairs were found in a flea market in Paris.

The first thing one notices in Codikow's living room is the unobstructed floor-to-ceiling view of Beverly Hills, visible through pivoting glass doors that are framed in rusted metal. The timeless black leather club chair is by Le Corbusier.

The bright red master bath with wide-planked wood floors is vibrant, soaked with California sunlight. The stained-glass window and custom steam shower—complete with cutout window and views of the Sunset Strip—contribute to the completely over-the-top feel.

Codikow believes that "we travel to both find ourselves and lose ourselves." During one of his many trips to Paris, he discovered the grandfather clock. A heavy wood door found in a downtown L.A. warehouse was mounted on a track and slides back and forth as a kitchen door. Codikow created the island out of pieces taken from a metal and antiques shop in Silverlake.

With all of the books, the old stone fireplace, vintage carpet, and Jean Cocteau drawing on the mantel, it's almost like being in a cozy Parisian flat—but right outside the windows of this master bedroom is a view that stretches from the skyscrapers of downtown Los Angeles all the way to the office buildings of Century City.

Kerry Brown and Stacey Sher admit to living a kind of gypsy lifestyle, with a constant mix of creative types—writers, actors, musicians—floating through the house. Brown often sits at the piano to serenade guests.

When producer and partner in Double Feature Films Stacey Sher (*Skeleton Key, Along Came Polly*) and musician Kerry Brown were looking for a house, they wanted one that would suit not only their immediate family but also the extended artistic "tribe" of filmmakers, writers, and musicians who regularly infuse and inspire their lives. The couple has two children (Tyler and Maggie) so space and comfort were of the utmost importance. In fact, before selling them the house, the previous owners made Sher and Brown promise that they would raise a family there (as the owners had for over twenty years in the home). Designed by renowned L.A. architect Wallace Neff as a retirement home for Myrtle A. Horenstein, the Coldwater Canyon house was once inhabited by another Hollywood couple known for their ever-expanding circle of family and friends in the film, television, and music industry: Julie Andrews and Blake Edwards.

Winner of an American Institute of Architects Award in 1955, while owned by fitness guru Vic Tanney, the house became Sher and Brown's in 2000. Although it had been sitting empty for about a year and was quite run down, Brown, a graduate in art and design from the Art Institute of Chicago, could see its potential the second they drove up to it. "If a house has got good energy and good bones, then it doesn't matter what else is going on," Brown says. Obsessed with renovation and a self-professed addict to HGTV, Brown knew that there was really no way they were going to bring the house back to the original Neff design. The house was originally built as a three-thousand-square-foot single gable, but because of the various additions that had been made over the years it was now seven thousand square feet and definitely not single gable anymore. Instead, Brown planned to move forward by finding whatever was left of the original design and exposing or showcasing it as close to the original way as he could. Recognizing that they had a unique Neff house—"It is a house that is an homage to the modernists but is still very warm"—the couple worked to merge the desire to be true to Neff's original design but with the requirements of their family-living lifestyle. "We really have the best of both worlds," says Sher.

What really sold Brown on the house were the three "really cool old-school" carved wooden palm trees that are structural to the house. Although they had been painted and repainted by previous owners, Brown loved that they had been carved specifically for the house. He stripped and stained them and now they are painted to look like real palm trees, which would be more in line with Neff's original plan. Brown loves Neff's craftsmanship and attention to detail and his ability to bring nature and the elements into his designs. "Neff would use a lot of exposed wood and earthy materials in his design that other architects would have hidden," says Brown. Chimneys were very organic, sometimes even suspended in the middle of the room, and rafters would remain exposed so you could see the actual structure of the house in the finished project. At the time, as Brown says, these ideas were "a little bit left of the dial. What I find interesting about Neff is his ability to marry the early Spanish architectural style that was going on in the early 1900s in California with the grandness of the Tuscan villa."

To guide them in the restoration/renovation, the couple got copies of the original blueprints for the house from the Huntington Library, which keeps the originals of all of Neff's designs. Brown had considerable experience designing and building state-of-the-art recording studios and renovating houses, so he took on much of the structural restoration himself. The restoration, however, was not without its discoveries or, as Brown so aptly puts it, its "happy accidents." It is not often that you sledgehammer a wall and discover an original eighteen-foot fireplace that had been plastered and dry-walled over years before. Brown completely restored it from an old photograph. When Brown and Sher initially looked at the house, the "magical" thirty-five-foot-high waterfall out in the courtyard was dry. On sight, Brown knew he could and would make it work again. The first day they got into the house, Brown was out, up to his knees in mud, digging the waterfall out, determined to restore it to what it once was. "It is now on twenty-four hours a day and is a source of great joy for us," Sher says.

Other renovations included pushing the front of the house out to add an entrance with new doors and moving a Neff-built staircase from the outside in. With these renovations, the house could be completely opened up for flow.

Fluidity and comfort play an integral role in the interior decor, which the couple took on without an interior designer. They both admit to having "a sort of gypsy thing" so there are always a lot of people around, coming to stay, and so on. "We wanted everyone to feel comfortable here," says Sher. It was important to them that the living space not seem regimented, that it would instead create a warm and stimulating environment for them and their children.

Sher and Brown's careers have also had an influence on the decor of the house. There are a pair of French iron chairs in the courtyard in the front of the house, where they often have dinner parties, that were found on the couple's trip to France for the European premiere of *Erin Brockovich,* a film Sher and her partner, Michael Shamberg, produced. There is a Swedron sofa in the guesthouse that Stacey discovered on a trip scouting locations for *Along Came Polly.* Numerous rock photographs adorn the walls of their media room, a room that Brown designed from top to bottom. Their photo collection is "99 percent black and white photographs of rock stars or artists like Andy Warhol," and ironically his favorite is the one color photograph that they have—a photograph of Bob Dylan the day he went electric for the first time in front of a crowd. The image of a "folk guy," which hangs among very loud and very electric rock icons like Led Zeppelin, the Who, and the Clash, is the focal point of the room.

Unusual for Los Angeles, the house sits on a two-acre parcel of land. The original Neff parcel was smaller, but subsequent owners like society doyenne Ames Cushing expanded it to include a guesthouse, pool, pool house, and back play yard. Sher and Brown have taken full advantage of the increased space and have hosted numerous parties around the pool—book launch parties, birthday parties, and film parties. Brown, who can seemingly build anything, recently completed a firehouse for their son, Tyler, who is obsessed with fire engines and now has his very own pole to slide down. Not to be outdone by those HGTV folks, Brown also built himself a two-thousand-square-foot full workshop for everything from woodwork to ceramics.

Stacey Sher and Kerry Brown are happy that the end result of their renovation to their architectural house is not only a great family home but also a home that is uniquely theirs. They enjoy the spacious and peaceful nature of the house and its surroundings, which give them "a sort of serenity that makes you feel like you're in the country," says Sher. They especially love the sound of the waterfall outside. The sliding glass doors that lead to the front of the house open and the waterfall can be heard throughout the whole space. In a city like Los Angeles, with demanding successful careers, children, and lives full of activity, it is essential to be able to have a retreat. The Sher/Brown house is just that and then some.

Previous owners had plastered over the original fireplace, so Sher and Brown re-created it from a picture they found in a book about Neff's designs. Black and white photographs by legendary artists Robert Doisneau, Henri Cartier-Bresson, and Andy Warhol are displayed above the mantel. The antique Persian rug is sentimental as it previously belonged to Stacey's grandmother. Sher and Brown found the cool vintage space chair covered in tan velvet at a store in Silverlake.

Built in 1953 for Myrtle A. Horenstein, Neff designed the house under a single sweeping gable, as seen in the original facade. The home won an Honor Award from the Southern California American Institute of Architects in 1955.

Some Angelenos bring the outside in; Sher and Brown decided to take the inside out. The family hangs out on a terrace off of the living room, covered with Oriental rugs and a mahogany Balinese bed with oversized leopard pillows. Brown converted a Gothic elevator door into the glass-topped coffee table, over which a vintage light from Dialogica is suspended.

The front patio is an oasis of black and gold bamboo, with a serene waterfall and Buddha statue, a gift from Sher's late mentor, Debra Hill. A Balinese pavilion, where the family enjoys eating dinner during the summer, can be seen at right. The patio has been the scene of many cocktail parties to celebrate everything from one of Sher's movie premieres to a book launch for good friend and author Carol Wolper.

Previously owned by Julie Andrews and Blake Edwards, the property sits on two acres. The kids' play area includes a life-sized dollhouse, tennis court, and pool—and is the perfect place to entertain. "We had Tyler's birthday party in the backyard, complete with real-life firefighters doing a demonstration," says Stacey. "Maggie prefers tea parties in the dollhouse." Other soirees held there include a fete for Richard LaGravenese's Emmy nomination and a caviar party out by the pool for the real-life Erin Brockovich.

Brown's "Coldwater Studio" is filled with guitars, recording and mixing equipment, and dozens of rock 'n' roll photos. He has produced songs for hit bands such as the Smashing Pumpkins, Cheap Trick, and his own group, Catherine, as well as composed tracks for the movies *Scream*, *Blow*, and *Walking and Talking*.

The whimsical carved wood palm trees are the most eye-catching original element in the home. Brown renovated much of the house himself, painting the trees and adding new mahogany and cherrywood floors. Native American oak chairs by Mission and Crafts specialist Gustav Stickley are paired with an oak table. Lining the walls in the dining room are Ed Ruscha photos from his "Sunset Strip" series, which have forever preserved the tackiness of the strip in the 1960s.

It would be interesting to know what Neff might think of the fact that the garage he designed for the house was transformed into an incredible screening room, filled with La-Z-Boys. The walls are covered in chocolate padded silk velvet and photographs of rock 'n' roll stars by Bob Gruen. Sher threw a party here for director Todd Haynes when his movie *Far from Heaven* came out. Most shocking for the family of a top Hollywood producer: Sher, Brown, and the kids get most excited watching Lakers games, not movies, in the screening room.

The elegant entrance was added by Sher and Brown when they pushed the house out a bit, though the integrity of Neff's original design is still unmistakable. Brown installed new doors made from stained and leaded glass windows found at Marc Tuna in Los Angeles, which bathe the area in sunlight. A vintage leather rug ties together the earthy tones in the entrance.

Neff built the staircase leading to the second floor and master suite outside—Sher and Brown moved it in, enclosing it in a double-height wall of windows, which looks out over the courtyard. A plaster statue of Joan of Arc that Sher found at an estate sale over twenty years ago stands watch.

"Fashion people all secretly love excess," declares Elizabeth Stewart. "They might say they worship Jil Sander and minimalism—but they're all closet aesthetes."

Something of an anomaly herself, Stewart has a serious New York fashion pedigree—she is the L.A.-based stylist and West Coast editor-at-large for the *New York Times Magazine* who formerly worked at *Women's Wear Daily* (*WDD*) in Paris and New York—but lives a happy family life in Santa Monica, California. Somehow she manages to juggle fashion week trips to New York, Milan, and Paris; she shoots all over the world with major fashion photographers; styles celebrities like Calista Flockhart and Kristin Davis for Hollywood award shows; and still maintains a fairly normal down-to-earth family life with her L.A.-based husband, Rob Braegin (a TV writer and producer responsible for *Murphy Brown* who now has development deals with Sony, Warner Bros. Television, and producer Jerry Bruckheimer), and two children, Ivy (age seven) and Ben (age five).

But her house on a cozy, pretty street in Santa Monica was, as she so eloquently puts it, "plain toast—normal" until Stewart put her fashion-person magic touch on it. She and her husband hired architect David Applebaum, best known for designing homes for Diane Keaton, Bob Hope, and Rupert Murdoch, to add on two rooms and to "make the exterior and interior seem as Old Spanish as possible." Inside, it's now an eclectic, magical mix of Moroccan tile, curtains made from Indian wedding saris, warm prints, and crystal chandeliers ("It's all about crystal chandeliers! I even have one in my daughter's bedroom. I'd put one in every room of the house if I could," Stewart exclaims). The home reflects Stewart's many loves and many sides: travel, romance, luxe, pattern, and texture. "Texture upon texture upon texture," she laughs. "I just went to the Etro store in Beverly Hills and got two throw pillows. I like a lot to look at."

As for her love of fashion—well, "my house is completely my fashion sense. I'm obsessed with Dries Van Noten and Etro. I love Missoni. There's a fashion pilgrimage that every fashion person *has* to take. That's to India. I took the required trip when I worked for *WWD*. I went to Rajasthan. The colors, the textiles—they're all really rich. It changes your eye. I wanted my house to be that. I shipped stuff back, and a lot of it didn't get here until six months later. And when I lived in Paris, Morocco is the Florida of Europe, so I went there a lot. That's another fashion person graduation trip. A lot of European fashionistas even have houses there."

After Europe, she lived in typical tiny New York spaces, saving up all the great things she'd found in India and Morocco, eventually meeting Braegin, and moving to Los Angeles. "When I met Rob, he had this perfect pristine 1920s Hollywood bungalow, done totally in bungalow style. Our only real problem was that he flew on United and I flew on American. We have a mixed mileage marriage—that's more of a problem than any design element." They purchased the Santa Monica house in 1998.

To help with the house, Stewart also enlisted her next-door neighbor—who just happened to be one of the hippest L.A. decorators. "It's funny," she says, "Katie McGloin's so hot right now. When she moved next door to me, I'd just started decorating on my own. I saw her house and said, 'This is *my* house—we have the same taste!' She knew where to go to find the things I wanted. We designed a fireplace in tile like one I'd seen in Morocco. Katie and I designed the tile together that I used on my steps and had it made. I like dark rich colors like reds and burgundy, but she kept saying, 'Throw in some freshness.' So we added white here and there. And I put sheepskin throws everywhere. I like a little bit of wit in my shoots and the pictures I style—and you can see that in my house, too."

But her favorite thing about the house is the small blue-walled room they call the study, opposite the dining room. "It looks like a little jewel box," says Stewart. "I'm totally into color—I'm always looking at fabric and texture for my job. I'm used to looking at strong color combinations. And I love any room that gives me an excuse for a vintage chandelier."

In the last few years her home has been the scene of a number of indoor/outdoor Moroccan-themed parties, including one for the shoe scion James Ferragamo, visiting from Florence (attended by various starlets, stars, fashion photogs, and denizens of the L.A.

charities Stewart devotes much time to); her own birthday soiree; lunches and small dinners for committee members of P.S. Arts (a charity that gives money to public school arts programs); and "The Bag Lunch" (a big once-a-year Hollywood event, where Stewart gets design houses to donate bags to auction off for charity).

For all of Stewart's love of romantic style—embellishment, embroidery, sparkle ("A sequin throw pillow is my dream")—she doesn't particularly dress that way, preferring to add touches of Balenciaga to more basic pieces, or wearing a hippie-style handbag with a vintage Halston goddess gown, or high Louboutin pumps with a simple black skirt. "It's true," she sighs. "I don't dress as Moroccany as my house. And you know why? I'm lazy. I'll put one fab piece on, then stop. My house is all layered up. But in clothes I prefer one layer. That's how it doesn't directly translate. My house is a better dresser than I am! But I told you, I like eclecticism. That's again true of fashion people. You take one vintage piece, one designer piece, one basic. It's highly personal. And it's all in the mix."

She may be a bit of a fish out of water living in Los Angeles, but in many ways it offers her the best of all worlds. "I love traveling to Paris, Milan, and New York, seeing fashion shows there, seeing the whole fashion crowd. But I love coming home to L.A.—and this house. It has the beauty of Italy, wines almost as good as France—and the New York designers are spending a lot more time here than they used to. Plus, I can dress down here and no one will give me a hard time!"

Previous page: Black and white photographs by famed fashion photographer Melvin Sokolsky hang above the Lillian Lageyre couch in Stewart's cozy library. Stewart found the vintage crystal chandelier in a Paris flea market.

Stewart and her children, Ivy and Ben, play in Ivy's room. Both the headboard and dust ruffle were custom-made with gorgeous fabric from India, including the velvet siding for the headboard.

In the master bedroom the stately maple sleigh bed, covered with Frette duvet and linens, faces onto a charming terrace overlooking the backyard and pool. Curtains custom-made with fabric from Donghia and a small table from Mexico add charm to the room.

Stewart supports local L.A. designers, like Tree, who made her red dress.

The Moroccan-style dining room features a Lillian Lageyre table and chairs and curtains made from rich fabric Stewart found on one of her many trips to India. The ceiling is painted deep blue giving guests the feeling they are eating outside.

The sunny double-height foyer includes a framed piece of Indian fabric and a black and white photograph by one of Stewart's favorite photographers, Christian Witkin. In the living room, visible through the arch, a custom wood and mirror coffee table and a fireplace framed with exquisite tiles from Morocco warm the light-filled space.

Architect John Lautner's work emphasized the relationship between humans, their homes, and the nature around them. In other words, where a house is located within its environment is just as important as the house itself. Having grown up in the Joshua Tree desert area of California, Brent Bolthouse, one of L.A.'s hottest nightclub/restaurant/event promoters, also knows a thing or two about environment. In fact, Bolthouse, the gatekeeper of L.A. nightlife for the past fifteen years, is all about environment and "its immense importance in all aspects of our lives."

From the strictly A-list parties he throws for clients (such as *Maxim, Vanity Fair,* Jennifer Lopez, Leonardo DiCaprio, and Sony PlayStation) to the nightclubs where he has been either promoter or owner (Avalon, Viper Room, Joseph's, and Body English at the Hard Rock Hotel Las Vegas), Bolthouse has an almost unparalleled reputation for creating environments that balance the kinetic energy of the world's hottest celebrities, trendsetters, and industry players in an interior decor that neither crowds nor overwhelms. Each of the venues reflects a conscious but seemingly effortless focus on making sure that people can feel like they are in an exclusive space yet are also able to move around and be

social. Though creating a balance between intimacy and flow is fundamental to Bolthouse's life and work, it was a bit of luck that led Bolthouse to the Lautner house in which he and his fiancée, Emma Heming, now reside.

Bolthouse first heard about the house from his real estate broker but was told that there were rumors going around the real estate community at the time that a sale of the house would be complicated because of an internal family conflict. Bolthouse, a longtime Lautner fan, knew, however, that if nothing else, he wanted to get in to see it. As luck would have it, not only was his future house for sale but so was the one next door. Lautner had built two houses on the same lot and Bolthouse had to decide which one he wanted. Knowing that he would renovate any house he bought, the challenge of being able to renovate and restore a Lautner house (this one, much to Heming's dismay, had shag carpeting and cottage cheese ceilings) was really an opportunity too good to pass up. Bolthouse saw the potential. "The house with its great lines is so unique and not something you see everyday. I feel so lucky that I found this important piece of architectural history." In January 2005, Bolthouse and Heming (up to the challenge herself) set to work renovating the first house he had heard about.

Once Bolthouse and Heming saw the original blueprints from the Lautner Foundation, they realized that the previous owners had done extensive work on the house that was not true to the initial Lautner design. Named for the original owners, the Polin House had skylights covered up, misplaced bathrooms added, and a completely redesigned dining room that interrupted the original aesthetic of the house. Allegedly, they had completely redone the whole house owing to some sort of falling out with Lautner himself. Bolthouse was able to find photographs taken of the house by artist Julian Schnabel (originally thought to be of the house next door) and that helped guide him during the renovation.

Working with contractor Rob Whitbread, Bolthouse had the house completely gutted so that the restoration could be as faithful to the original plans as possible. As he says, "The house today has more Lautner in it than it ever has." Though restoration of an architectural house can be unimaginably difficult and expensive, it is often more rewarding than not. As a result of Bolthouse's great instinct, such was the case with the dining room in his beloved Lautner—in some ways kind of a mystery to him—one that kept evolving and revealing itself. At the beginning of the restoration, Bolthouse had some very definite ideas about changes he wanted to make to the dining room. At the last minute, he decided to refurbish it exactly the way the original plans read, feeling like it was the right way to be true to the house. "I am so glad I did it this way. It couldn't have been any better," Bolthouse admits.

Though Bolthouse and Heming have done some upgrades—most notably the kitchen—they really brought the focus of the house back to the versatility of the indoor/outdoor living space that Lautner specialized in. The glass windows and doors now slide open and shut the way they were intended, creating a feeling of a much bigger, more open house than its fifteen hundred square feet. Bolthouse is no stranger to construction or design: he had two restaurants in the 1990s, Babylon and the Coffee House, that he designed himself from soup to nuts. He knows what he likes and as a photographer (for the past five years), he has an instinctually good eye. Though he cites Salvador Dalí as a favorite artist and Morocco as a big inspiration, Bolthouse has an innate knowledge of space and perspective. He can look inside an empty space or lens and know how to create a

composition without sacrificing the integrity of its elements.

Bolthouse was very conscious of using the house as his guide for the interior decor. He used a mixture of trademark Lautner natural elements—concrete, brick, glass, and redwood—in the architecture of the house to serve as a backdrop that would complement, not compete against, the furniture he chose. "If you have a Spanish house, it would seem odd to me to make the interior ultramodern. You can have modern pieces but you can't put all Danish furniture in a Spanish house. It just doesn't work." Bolthouse did not want his house to feel fragmented or cold, so with the help of interior designer Frank X. Medrano and his associate, Steve Brabson, he looked for pieces that had warmth to them, much like the house itself. The key to a great home for him is, "a house that is carefully designed . . . something that is thought out from beginning to end."

With its openness and space, the house has a great calming influence on Bolthouse and Heming, whose professional lives are pretty chaotic. (Heming is a top fashion model for companies such as Victoria's Secret and an actress. She can be seen in an upcoming movie with Bruce Willis and Halle Barry.) They can come home and connect to nature (deer regularly come through their yard) in a way that doesn't exist in most urban places. To them it is one of the many great things about living in Los Angeles. "Not only is the quality of life in L.A. so great, but the weather is fantastic. Los Angeles has been very good to me," says Bolthouse. About the first residence that he has ever owned, complete with a deck perfect for entertaining and views of the city and the hills, he says, "I feel extremely lucky that I have found a place that really does embellish the California dream."

Previous page: Both Bolthouse and Heming are avid photography buffs. Emma also has a keen interest in and eye for real estate; she owns homes in her native Malta, New York, London, and Miami. The octagonal frame, slanted windows and top-of-the-world views give the house a spaceship feel. Poured into the concrete floors are copper pipes that give the house radiant heat, split into separate zones for each room.

High in the hills near Mulholland, the house features staggering views of nearly the entire valley. Bolthouse and Heming completely gutted the home after purchasing it in late 2004, rebuilding it the way Lautner would have wanted, by using the original sketches. "We did as much as we could to keep the integrity of the house," Bolthouse says. It is hard to believe that the dramatic deck was once enclosed in gray wood.

"I feel so lucky that I found this important piece of architectural history."

The movement from indoor to outdoor space is seamless. The continuous design and large steel-covered glass doors that slide back create that unique L.A. sense of alfresco living indoors. Metal Harry Bertoia chairs paired with a metal and glass-topped table grace the deck, where guests can kick back and take in the extreme view.

The original triangular skylight in the study had been covered in wood by the former owner and not until Bolthouse obtained the homes' sketches from the Lautner Foundation did he even realize that it existed. In addition, he restored the poured concrete walls, which had also been covered in wood, and had to pull up shag carpet and tile to find the original concrete floors. The vintage teak furniture is from Denmark 50 and the groovy white lamp is by Jonathan Adler.

The house was built in 1947 for Lautner's contractor and his family. In the expansive living room are the red-wood walls that Bolthouse restored, as well as the original brick fireplace. The brick wall once accommodated a large built-in fish tank. Old meets new in vintage teak chairs with woven-wool cushions and a stainless-steel glass-topped cocktail table.

Interior designer Frank X. Medrano and his associate, Steve Brabson, assisted Bolthouse in selecting mostly vintage teak furniture, including the Danish dining-room table and chairs. All of the windows, which open to the backyard, are original to the house, though Bolthouse and Heming did extend the far wall to add a bit of space. Blending in with the ivy-covered landscaping is a 1950s glass and chrome light fixture hanging from the ceiling.

Bolthouse and Heming worked tirelessly on the renovation, attending to every detail from searching stone yards for the exact granite for the kitchen, to redrawing the sketches of the space for furniture placement.

Windows cut out near the redwood ceiling frame the master bath and allow sunlight to stream in. The original tub was taken out to provide more room and a Euro Concepts stylish double basin was added. The result is simplicity that transcends a specific era.

Intimate entertaining at home will be quite a contrast to their day jobs: Bolthouse as a successful Hollywood event promoter and Heming as a top fashion model. Their renovation shows off the unembellished lines of the house and the natural materials used, such as redwood and concrete.

A chic vintage teakwood desk and matching chair perfectly suit the redwood walls in the study.

Ask anyone living in Los Angeles about finding the right house and they will tell you what an absolute nightmare it can be. But, as with many things in life, you can get lucky just when you are about to throw in the towel and discover a gem that you weren't even looking for in the first place.

Mary Parent, the former vice chair of Worldwide Production for Universal Pictures, found just that gem in the Brentwood section of Los Angeles. With her insanely hectic schedule (which has included the production of multiple slates of movies every year), she was hoping to find the perfect "move-in ready" home. Parent had looked at a number of different potential homes in her search, all of which were either too small or too dark, with little or no outside space for the recent addition to her life—her puppy. Other places that might have worked for her had been significantly refurbished with elements like marble that really didn't suit her taste or lifestyle. Parent, therefore, resigned herself to the fact that even the "right" house would certainly need work done to it. She was ready to face renovations. But the minute Parent walked into the Brentwood house, she knew that she really loved it. Not only did this house have everything she needed, but it had a key quality she had been looking for without success—a tremendous amount of space and light. The other major attraction of the house was the shocking surprise that it needed almost no renovation.

The Brentwood house was ready for its close-up upon move in. Built in 1937, the residence had originally been a barn and carriage house attached to a large estate farther up the hill. The original owners were Dr. and Mrs. Rex Ross. He was a sort of "doctor to the stars" in his day and the chief of vascular surgery at what was then Hollywood Presbyterian and Santa Monica Hospitals. The owners before Parent, producer Michael Manheim and his wife, had purchased the house from the Rosses and restored it perfectly with much of its original craftsmanship. Manheim also installed a brand-new kitchen, renovated all of the bathrooms, and added about one thousand square feet, which makes the house feel open and airy and gives it the loft-like quality that Parent calls "my own little paradise."

Though there is some landscaping that she would still like to do, the few renovations that Parent has made so far were much more motivated by the nature of her job than by flaws in the house. She installed a state-of-the-art media room in what used to be a horse stall. (A true Hollywood film executive, Parent has a top-of-the-line technology system that stores over two thousand films on DVD.) She also widened the driveway as she admits that she is invariably in a bit of a hurry. Parent is even thankful not to have to drive the treacherous "one car at a time" canyon roads in the hills of her former neighborhood. "I know it sounds too good to be true, but the house really is perfect," Parent says.

To decorate the "perfect" structure, Parent brought in interior designer Brad Dunning, who has created spaces for fashion guru Tom Ford and quintessential Hollywood couple Demi Moore and Ashton Kutcher. Dunning initially helped Parent achieve a space that has a cool eclectic sensibility to it without feeling "done." Parent wanted to respect the home's age and its history as a barn/carriage house. So she juxtaposed really old rustic—an 1880s stagecoach safe—with very specific modern pieces—a black marble coffee table—to give one the feeling that it had all been put together over time. The secret is that nothing is uncomfortable or too high maintenance. Though she used some lighter fabrics and some linen (and a few items in white), she generally looked for really durable decor. "I wanted guests to be able to eat/drink wherever and to be able to sit or put their feet up on the furniture," Parent explains. One of her favorite pieces of furniture in the house is an industrial metal cart by her bed. "It's highly functional with plenty of room to put books and magazines, and I never have to worry about it getting ruined with things like watermarks, candles, or pens." Parent has also worked with designer Tim Andreas, who was previously responsible for the design of many Ian Schrager hotels and is now working on homes in New York and Los Angeles. "Tim came with a slightly different view and eye that was interesting," she says.

Parent has lived in the house since January 2004 and hopes to make it not only a place to live, but a sanctuary. "For so long, I didn't pay that much attention to my house. It was just a pit stop to sleep [in]. Now to be able to come home at night is so great," she says. Very private and set quite a bit back from the street, the house offers a comfortable and peaceful environment where she can enjoy the little downtime that she has. The energy and the flow of the house are a true source of joy for Parent; she loves walking into a space "that just has a quality to it that makes you want to spend time and makes you feel comfortable and happy and relaxed." This means maximizing the indoor/outdoor living area including both the front courtyard and patio, which are accessed through great big glass doors. "I wanted [the interior] to flow and blend well with the outside foliage, so I used lots of neutrals, adding more colors in pillows, throws, and artwork." One of the things that she likes most about the house is that it reminds her of the open airy brightness so present in her experience growing up by the beach in Santa Barbara. "The minute I come home, I open the doors and windows because I don't like to feel closed in." During the many years she lived up in the Hollywood Hills, Parent often felt isolated and removed from things; now living in Brentwood, she feels that she has the best of both worlds—privacy without isolation. For her, this is the very best of city living and the epitome of the L.A. lifestyle.

The previous owner completely opened up the back of the house with a huge wall of windows that lead onto a patio. Near the original brick fireplace stands a Christian Liaigre table surrounded by chairs of mahogany and white canvas from Ligne Roset. The vintage chocolate leather chaise was a gift from manager Sandy Gallin, after he sold his Malibu home. A found 1930s Deco table in ash sits next to the chaise.

Many elements, such as the front door, make it obvious that Parent's home was once a barn and stable. Built in 1937, the house was originally part of an extremely large property owned by a third-generation L.A. doctor, Rex Ross.

For Parent, this is the very best of city living and the epitome of the L.A. lifestyle.

Parent selected dark wood pieces to match the ebonized floors. A black marble-topped coffee table by Lee Stanton is stacked with art books.

The fact that Parent's home was formerly a barn and stable gives it a very funky yet chic feel. The high-pitched beamed ceiling with skylights keeps the living room light and airy, a nice contrast to the original ebonized wood floors. Parent's choice of eclectic furnishings makes the laid-back space more sophisticated, as seen on the right, where an 1880s iron stagecoach safe from Blackman Cruz sits below a resin sculpture by Ron Diehl.

The back part of the house is a wall of windows that opens to a gorgeous brick patio and sun-drenched lawn. Parent selected primarily neutral and durable fabrics, with splashes of color thrown in with pillows, blankets, and artwork, so that the flow of the house would blend seamlessly with the exterior foliage.

Glass doors on the left of the long brick hallway lead out to the front lawn of the house. On the right, interior windows can be seen where horses used to poke their heads out of the former stalls—which now serve as Parent's screening room.

Light floods the master bedroom, streaming in the back wall of windows and the skylights overhead. A Deco-inspired custom-made four-post bed is the centerpiece.

An early-twentieth-century French lounge chair offers relaxation in the master bedroom. Black and white photographs hang on several of the walls, including a landscape image on the back wall, above the walnut dresser.

The old horse stalls make the perfect screening room for Parent, who oversaw ninety films as vice chairman of Worldwide Production at Universal Pictures, resulting in twenty Academy Award nominations and seven Oscars. Parent outfitted her home theater with the most advanced technology around—the Kaleidescape Server, which can store over two thousand films on DVD. Displayed in the highest quality, the server can play different movies simultaneously in various rooms of the house.

Jason Binn, CEO and founder of Niche Media, LLC, has built a veritable publishing empire based on the glamour associated with a certain lifestyle. With his publications such as *Los Angeles Confidential, Aspen Peak, Gotham, Hamptons, Boston Common,* and *Capitol File,* as well as the influential *Ocean Drive,* which he cofounded, Binn has tapped into a niche market by covering some of the most recognizable names in business, arts, entertainment, politics, and music. His big glossy magazines are "city-centric from an insider's perspective" and there is no greater insider than Binn himself. With some of Hollywood's biggest players and celebrities on his advisory board, from power agents Ed Limato, Jim Berkus, Patrick Whitesell, and Jim Wiatt to legendary producer Robert Evans to A-listers like Jennifer Lopez and Will Smith, Binn certainly knows a thing or two about what makes L.A. life tick.

Binn and his wife, Haley, split their time between Niche Media's respective markets. With no permanent home in Los Angeles, they have for the past few years "set up camp" in the Four Seasons Hotel Los Angeles. Located in a quiet residential neighborhood off of Burton Way, with its tropically landscaped rooftop pool, world-famous full service spa, and award-winning Gardens restaurant, the hotel is a mix of "European grace, Beverly Hills style, and relaxed California attitude, with a healthy dose of celebrity glamour thrown in," says Binn. It is this dynamic combination that brings him back to his suite there and to Los Angeles time and time again.

This energy, found only in Los Angeles, compelled Binn to launch what would become *Los Angeles Confidential.* "So much of what takes place in the country when you read any national lifestyle magazine—so much of the content, so much of the buzz that you read—is derived from Los Angeles. It seemed like a great place to create a magazine." With participation in charity events like Nancy Davis's Race to Erase, social functions like Wolfgang Puck's Los Angeles Food and Wine Festival, Los Angeles Fashion Week, and movie premieres like *Must Love Dogs,* starring Diane Lane and John Cusack, *Los Angeles Confidential* has direct access to the pulse of the L.A. lifestyle. The city provides the magazine with the opportunity to connect editorial content with events that are not as available in other markets. For example, the magazine has hosted Oscar parties with winners like Jamie Foxx and hosted Emmy parties with nominees like *Desperate Housewives'* Teri Hatcher. "Having Teri Hatcher on the cover and hosting an Emmy party with the magazine right before the Emmys is one of the special things that we can do in L.A. and not in any other market," Binn says.

One of the most talked about examples of this was *Los Angeles Confidential*'s 2002 launch, during which Binn "was fortunate enough to have Harvey Weinstein [one of Binn's partners in the magazine and former cochair of Miramax] introduce me to the city in conjunction with Miramax during Oscar week." Very well known for his prowess at marketing and publicity as well as for having the ear of everyone in Hollywood, Weinstein helped Binn place the brand new magazine in all of the VIP cars and planes that descend upon the city that week. For both Jason and the magazine, it was invaluable immediate access to all of the tastemakers, celebrities, and bigshots in Los Angeles. The icing on the cake was having Nicole Kidman on the cover of that issue—right in time to win an Oscar (for *The Hours*). "It was amazing and definitely one of the most talked about and exciting launches that I have ever had."

In addition to the A-list celebrity component, it was important for Binn to have a magazine that really celebrates Los Angeles and its vibrant and ever-changing community. "I feel like there are so many other publications around the country that mock or take shots at the people and lifestyle of L.A., so it was very important for my magazine to capture the beautiful people and places and celebrate the good things about the city," he says. For example, when *Los Angeles Confidential* covers a restaurant, bar, or hotel, if it is a bad review, the magazine does not publish it, as the point of the publication is to cover the places you should know about and go to. "It is exciting to have a magazine that connects to the community and celebrates it in an interactive way so readers can be a part of it," says Binn.

Los Angeles has a very low-key ambience that Binn loves, yet it is a place where he gets a tremendous amount of work done. "I like the relaxed pace and atmosphere of L.A., yet you are still around really serious people who work hard and take their lives seriously—personally and professionally," he says. Being from New York, where there are always moving objects—traffic, trains, cars, buses, bike messengers—Binn loves the fact that everyone starts their day really early in Los Angeles, and with the weather, water, and open air, it has an energy that makes everything feel fresh. One of the things Binn and his wife love to do when they are in Los Angeles is hike Runyon Canyon. "The canyon is one of the most unique things—a combination of vigorous exercise, great views, and of course, ubiquitous celebrity sightings—about Los Angeles

as a city," says Binn. "It makes us forget about everything."

Binn enjoys the incredible luxury of having all of his personal needs taken care of at his suite at the Four Seasons. Though it is not his home, it has all of a home's creature comforts and then some. Binn's favorite thing about the Four Seasons is the bar. "It is a great power scene—everyone goes through there at one point and time. It is also a wonderfully active room with fantastic service that is a great place to socialize," says Binn. He is particularly partial to the use of space in the room and likes the fact that "it is a cozy intimate place where you can be next to people or be around people but they are not on top of you. The energy is really special," he asserts.

Publishing lifestyle magazines in some of the most exciting and dynamic cities in the country affords Binn the opportunity to see and be influenced by a tremendous amount of design. A fan of bespoke suits, Binn's taste leans toward exceptionally well-made minimalist chic. He loves architects Frank Lloyd Wright and Richard Meier and the open airy halls, high ceilings, and light fabrics that allow the flood of sunlight to permeate the Four Seasons. He is also partial to the minimalist homes in Los Angeles that have that clean, open, and light aesthetic. Binn cites Darren Star's house, "the perfect combination of minimalism and chic" and the J. Paul Getty Museum at the Getty Center as good examples of that unique Los Angeles minimalism.

Binn strongly believes that "your environment has a major impact on your own personal style," whether it means being open to incorporating a design style into your home that you wouldn't normally embrace or living in a way that suits a particular climate. Indoor/outdoor living and practically year-round entertaining are very unique to Los Angeles and one of the reasons it is such a great place to live and play. For Binn, a perfect day in Los Angeles is spending time taking it all in. "What is great about L.A. is the different vibe of each neighborhood," he says. Whether it is Melrose, Beverly Hills, Runyon Canyon, the beach, the hotels, the museums, or the historic movie theaters, for Jason Binn, it is all quintessential L.A. living.

Previous page: Binn, pictured here in his usual suite, runs *Los Angeles Confidential, Gotham, Hamptons, Aspen Peak,* and new titles *Boston Common* and *Capitol File.*

An Erwin Binder bronze sculpture watches over the luxurious garden and oversized tile pool of fountains. An army of full-time gardeners plant and groom the grounds, exotic trees, plants, and shrubbery.

On the top floor of the Four Seasons, which is full of suites, a hand-painted sky blue ceiling greets VIP guests and gives one the feeling of being in an Italian palazzo. The walnut console was custom-made and the glittering crystal chandelier was imported from Italy. Celebrity florist Eric Buterbaugh, whose shop is right in the hotel, designs all of its exquisite arrangements.

The double-wide living and dining room is the perfect place for Binn to entertain clients while on the West Coast. The suite has that perfect L.A. mix of being elegant yet comfortable. The woven wool carpet is from Stark. Rattan dining-room table and chairs were found at McGuire Furniture and the iron and glass-top coffee table, with requisite copies of *Los Angeles Confidential* displayed, was custom-made by Murray's Iron Works.

Constantly networking on his cell phone or BlackBerry, Binn keeps in close touch with Hollywood pals like actor Adrien Brody, director Brett Ratner, and L.A. chief of police Bill Bratton.

Shimmering hand-laid Bisazza glass mosaic tile, with a maple vanity and accents on the oversized soaking tub, add opulence in the master bath. Binn can tune into CNBC for stock market updates on his flat-screen TV, mounted next to the steam shower, as he gets ready for the day.

Binn's sitting room leads into a luxurious bedroom, complete with canopied bed from the Silk Trading Company. The Four Seasons uses only the finest artisans to fabricate pieces for their suites, like the Mark David side chair made with Spinneybeck leather.

Celebrities visiting L.A. can often be spotted by the pool or taking a swim.
The pool cabanas are used for relaxation or to get a message.

Binn and his *Los Angeles Confidential* staff often convene to select cover shots in the ornate and quiet sitting area next to the lobby. Intra Design conceived and decorated the space to reflect "an eclectic mix of comfortable styles rather than just traditional Californian style."

At the elevator bank, the Italian handpainted marble floor adds to the sense of luxury and opulence that the hotel is so known for.

Use this guide to locate many of the pieces of furniture, textiles, accessories, lighting fixtures and fashion in the book. Many of the large retailers are located in major cities across the country, so check your local listing. For vintage pieces, please check with dealers, galleries, and the large auction houses, like Sotheby's and Christie's.

Furniture, Home Accessories, Textiles, Interior Designers, Home Retailers, Architects, Landscape Designers, Flea Markets

Alvar Aalto
www.hermanmiller.com;
www.aalto.com
Galleries, select dealers, and
auction houses worldwide
Home furnishings

Andromeda International
www.andromedamurano.it
Glass lighting

Ann Sacks
www.annsacks.com
800-278-TILE
Tile, stone, plumbing, lighting

Architectural Pottery
www.architecturalpottery.com
Sold at California Living,
323-930-2601
Pottery

Art Luna Landscaping
Art Luna Salon
2116 Main St.
Santa Monica, CA
310-450-7168
Landscaping, garden design

Aubusson Carpet
www.aubusson-carpets.com
Galleries, select dealers and
auction houses worldwide
Carpets

B&B Italia
www.bebitalia.it
800-872-1697
Home furnishings, accessories

Baker Furniture
www.kohlerinteriors.com
800-59-BAKER
Home furnishings, upholstery

Bauer Pottery
www.bauerpottery.com
888-213-0800
Ceramic pottery

Billy Haines
Galleries, select dealers and
auction houses worldwide
Home furnishings

Blackman Cruz
www.blackmancruz.com
800 La Cienega
Los Angeles, CA
310-657-9228
Home furnishings and lighting

Bradbury
707-746-6262
Wall upholstery

Brenda Antin
1021 Montana Ave.
Santa Monica, CA
310-393-0042
Interior design, home furnishings

Bruno Mathsson
Galleries, select dealers and
auction houses worldwide
Pernilla chair

Bugatti
www.bugatti.com
Leather goods

California Living
601 N. LaBrea Ave.
Los Angeles, CA
323-930-2601
*Home furnishings, accessories,
pottery*

Charles Allem
www.charlesallem.com
cpa@charlesallemdesigns.com
Interior design

Charles and Ray Eames
www.hermanmiller.com and select
dealers worldwide
Home furnishings

Chelsea Editions
www.chelseatextiles.com
212-758-0005
*Antique textiles, cushions,
furnishings*

Chinese Jesus
www.chinesejesus.com
310-821-9112
Home furnishings

Chris Lehrecke for Ralph Pucci
www.ralphpucci.com
212-633-0452
Furniture

Christian Liaigre/Holly Hunt
www.hollyhunt.com
312-329-5999
Home furnishings, textiles, leather

Colin Cowie
www.colincowie.com
9663 Santa Monica Boulevard
Suite 317
Beverly Hills, CA
and
80 Fifth Avenue
Suite 1004
New York, NY
Parties, wedding, home furnishings

Cowtan and Tout Fabric
8687 Melrose Ave., B647
Los Angeles, CA
310-659-1423
Fabric and textiles

David Cressey Planter
www.architecturalpottery.com
Planters and containers

Decades
www.decadesinc.com
8214 Melrose Ave.
Los Angeles, CA
323-655-1960
*Vintage clothes, bags, shoes, and
accessories*

Denmark 50
www.denmark50.com
7974 Melrose Ave.
Los Angeles, CA
323-650-5222
Danish modern furniture

Dialogica
www.dialogica.com
8820 Beverly Blvd.
Los Angeles, CA
310-888-0008
Home furnishings

Diane Resenstein + Bret Wilke
Russell Simpson Company
West Hollywood, CA
323-651-3992
Interior design

DIVA-LA
www.diva.com
8801 Beverly Blvd.
Los Angeles, CA
310-278-3191
Home furnishings, lighting,
accessories

Donghia
www.donghia.com
212-925-2777
Home furnishings, textiles

Ed Hardy
www.edhardysf.com
415-626-6300
Antique furniture, decorative arts

Edward Fields
www.edwardfields.com
310-652-3058
Rugs and carpets

Edward Wormley
www.collectdunbar.com
336-734-1700
Midcentury home furnishings

Eero Saarinen
www.retroathome.com
510-658-6600
Home furnishings

Eileen Gray
www.moderncollections.com and
other online dealers
Transit chair

Eric Buterbaugh
300 South Doheny Dr.
Los Angeles, CA
310-247-7120
Florist

Ernest Batchelder
Galleries, select dealers and
auction houses worldwide
Decorative tiles, pottery

Etro
www.etro.com
461 North Rodeo Drive
Beverly Hills, CA 90210
310-248-2855
212-317-9096
Clothing, accessories, home
furnishings, fabrics

Euro Concepts
8687 Melrose Ave., B-119
Los Angeles, CA
310-274-5896
Bath design, fixtures

Fendi
www.fendi.com
310-276-8888
Clothing, home furnishings,
accessories

Fortuny Fabrics
www.fortuny.com
310-657-7150
212-753-7153
Fabrics

Four Seasons Hotel
www.fourseasons.com
300 S. Doheny Dr.
Los Angeles, CA
310-273-2222
Luxury hotels

Frette
www.frette.com
212-299-0424
Linens, homewear, fragrances

George Nelson
Galleries, select dealers and
auction houses worldwide
Home furnishings

Gervasoni and Bolla Lamps
www.gervasoni1882.com
011 39 43265 6611 (Italy)
info@gervasoni1882.com
Contemporary furniture, lighting

Gio Ponti
www.gioponti.com
888-NPONTI-1
Midcentury home furnishings,
lighting, accessories

Gladding McBean Pottery
www.gladdingmcbean.paccoast.com
800-776-1133
Ceramic pottery

Greta Grossman
Galleries, select dealers and
auction houses worldwide
Midcentury furniture, lighting

Gustav Stickley
www.gustavstickley.com
Galleries, select dealers and
auction houses worldwide
Furniture, pottery, accessories

Hans Wegner
www.hans_wegner.kolmorgen.com
Galleries, select dealers and
auction houses worldwide
Danish furniture

Harry Bertoia Chairs
Galleries, select dealers and
auction houses worldwide
Wire chairs

Harvey Probber
Galleries, select dealers and
auction houses worldwide
Midcentury home furnishings

Herman Miller
www.hermanmiller.com
888-443-4357; 800-646-4400
Home furnishings, architecture,
designer

Hoffman Leather Chairs
Galleries, select dealers and
auction houses worldwide
Art deco furniture

Hollyhock
Suzanne Rheinstein
214 N. Larchmont
West Hollywood, CA
310-777-0100
323-463-3081
Interior design, home furnishings,
lifestyle store

Holly Hunt
www.hollyhunt.com
312-329-5999
Home furnishings, textiles,
leathers

Ian Walmsley Design
3825 Willat Ave. A
Culver City, CA
310-836-0772
Interior fabrication, woodwork
design

Isamu Noguchi
www.noguchi.org
Galleries, select dealers and
auction houses worldwide
Home furnishings

J. F. Chen
8414 Melrose Ave.
Los Angeles, CA
323-655-6310
Antiques and home furnishings

J. Robert Scott
www.jrobertscott.com
310-680-4200
Home furnishings and textiles

James Jennings
Galleries, select dealers and
auction houses worldwide
Home furnishings

Jay Griffiths Landscaping
310-392-5558
Landscaping

Jenny Armit
www.jennyarmit.com
323-653-3048
Interior decor

Jonathan Adler
www.jonathanadler.com
8125 Melrose Ave.
Los Angeles, CA
323-658-8390
Pottery, lighting, textiles, bedding, furniture

Jorgen Hovelskov
Galleries, select dealers and auction houses worldwide
Harp chair

Joseph Free
323-782-1790
Florist

Jules Leleu
Galleries and auction houses worldwide
Home furnishings

Karl Springer
www.matthewsandparker.com
310-854-3838
Home furnishings

Kasthall
www.kasthall.com
Rugs

Klein Reid
www.kleinreid.com
718-388-9331
Contemporary porcelain objects

Knoll
www.knoll.com
800-343-5665
Home and office furnishings

Lalique
www.lalique.com
310-271-7892
Crystal and glass objects, jewelry

Le Corbusier
www.foundationlecorbusier.assoc.com
Sold by dealers and at auction
Home furnishings

Lee Stanton
www.leestanton.com
310-855-9800
Antiques

Lillian Lageyre
1231 Montana Ave.
Santa Monica, CA
310-393-6408
Antique furniture and design

Lynn Weinberg
At auction and select dealers
Home furnishings

Manuel Canovas Fabric
www.manuelcanovas.com
310-659-1423
Fabrics, textiles

Marc Appleton
www.appleton-architects.com
310-828-0430
Architecture, design

Marché aux Puces
48, rue Jules Valles
Paris, just outside the 18th Arrondissement; generally cash only

Mark Harigian
www.harigianfitness.com
818-243-5132
Gym design and fitness equipment

Marmol Radziner
www.marmolradziner.com
310-826-6222
Architects and furniture designers

Martynus-Tripp Design
www.martynus-tripp.com
323-651-4445
Interior design, home furnishings

Mathieu Lustrerie
www.mathieufall.com
33-0390749-240
Chandeliers

McGuire Furniture
www.kohlerinteriors.com
800-662-4847
Home furnishings, lighting, textiles, accessories

Michel Cadestin
www.centrepompidou.fr
Galleries, select dealers and auction houses worldwide
Furniture

Mies van der Rohe
At auction and dealers
Home furnishings

Milo Baglioni
mbmilo@aol.com
323-851-7277
Interior design

Minotti
www.minotti.it
310-278-6851
Home furnishings, accessories

Müller Frères
Galleries, select dealers and auction houses worldwide
Lamps, chandeliers, glass objects

Murray's Iron Works
8632 Melrose Ave.
Los Angeles, CA
310-652-0632
Iron furniture and home accessories

Nancy Corzine
www.nancycorzine.com
310-652-4859; 212-223-8340
Home furnishings

Niermann Weeks
www.niermannweeks.com
310-659-6876
Home furnishings, lighting, textiles, accessories

Pasadena Swap Meet/ Rosebowl Flea Market
www.pasadena.com
1001 Rose Bowl Dr.
Pasadena, CA
323-560-SHOW
Second Sunday of every month

Paul Frankl
At auction and select dealers
Home furnishings

Paul Lazlo
www.retroathome.com
Home furnishings

Paul McCobb
www.retroathome.com
510-658-6600
Galleries, select dealers and auction houses worldwide
Midcentury home furnishings

Philippe Starck
www.philippe-starck.com
011 33 14807 5454 (France)
*Home furnishings, bathroom
fixtures, lighting, clothing*

Pratesi
www.pratesi.com
310-274-7661
Linens, home accessories, apparel

Ralph Lauren Home
www.polo.com
888-475-7674
*Home furnishings, bath, linens,
gifts, accessories*

Raymor by Ben Seibel
www.the1950s.com
Galleries, select dealers and
auction houses worldwide
*Furniture, dinnerware, home
accessories*

Reform Gallery
816 N. La Cienega Blvd.
Los Angeles, CA
310-854-1033
*Modernist home furnishings,
accessories*

Regen Projects
www.regenprojects.com
629 Almont Dr.
West Hollywood, CA
310-276-5424
Dealers of contemporary fine art

Retro Gallery
www.retroglass.com
1100 South LaBrea Ave.
Los Angeles, CA
323-936-5261
Glass, lamps, ceramics, books

Rietveld
www.gerritrietveld.com
Galleries, select dealers and
auction houses worldwide
Home furnishings

Rios Clementi Hale Studios
www.rchstudios.com
323-634-9220
Architecture, design

Robert Kuo Designs
www.robertkuo.com;
www.annsacks.com
8686 Melrose Ave.
Los Angeles, CA
310-855-1555
Bath design, accessories

Rogers & Goffigon Fabric
8687 Madison Ave.
Los Angeles, CA
310-659-1423
Fabrics, textiles

Room Service
8115 West Third St.
Los Angeles, CA
323-653-4242
Home furnishings, accessories

Rose Tarlow
www.rosetarlow.com
323-651-2202
Furniture, textiles

Scalamandré Fabric
www.scalamandre.com
718-361-8311
Fabric

Scott Flax
1660 Stanford St.
Santa Monica, CA
310-829-1445
Custom paintwork

Sellers & Josephson
800-238-9152
Wall coverings, textiles

Sergio Rodrigues
Galleries, select dealers and
auction houses worldwide
Contemporary furniture

Shelter
7920 Beverly Blvd.
Los Angeles, CA
323-937-3222
Home furnishings, accessories

Silk Trading Co.
www.silktrading.com
323-954-9280
Home furnishings, handbags, paint

Spinneybeck Leather
www.spinneybeck.com
800-482-7777
Upholstery leather

Stark Carpets
www.starkcarpets.com
212-752-9000
*Carpet, fabric, furnishings, wall
coverings*

Steven Slan/VIA
www.viarc.com
323-962-9101
Architecture, design

Studio 11
www.deniscolomb.com
1711 Sargent Pl.
Los Angeles, CA
213-250-1711
Architecture, design

Swan chairs
By Arne Jacobson
Galleries, select dealers and
auction houses worldwide

T. H. Robsjohn-Gibbings
Galleries, select dealers and
auction houses worldwide
Midcentury home furnishings

Teco Pottery
309-690-7966 (or at auction)
Ceramic pottery

Therien and Company
www.therien.com
310-657-4615
Home furnishings, lighting

Thonet
www.thonet.com
800-551-6702
Art Deco furniture

Tiffany & Company
www.tiffany.com
800-843-3269
Home accessories, jewelry, gifts

Timney Fowler
www.timneyfowler.com
London, England
020 8748 3010
Fabrics

Timorous Beasties
www.timorousbeasties.com
212-355-6241
Fabrics, wall coverings, accessories

Tommy Parzinger
Galleries, select dealers and
auction houses worldwide
Furniture, lighting

Tom Rael
Pleskow + Rael
www.pleskowrael.com
310-577-9300
Architects, furniture design

Tony Duquette Jewelry
At fine select retailers like
Bergdorf Goodman, Stanley
Korshak, and Geary's

Van Keppel Green
Select dealers and auction houses
worldwide
Home furnishings

Fashion Resources

Alice Temperley
www.temperleylondon.com
212-219-2929
Women

Azzedine Alaia
At Barneys New York and other
select retailers
Women

Balenciaga
www.balenciaga.com
212-206-0872
Women/Men

Banana Republic
www.bananarepublic.com
1-800-BR-STYLE
Women/Men

Chloé
www.chloe.com
212-717-8220
Women

Christian Dior Homme
www.dior.com
Men

Chrome Hearts
www.chromehearts.com
310-854-9800; 212-327-0707
Women/Men

Converse
www.converse.com
888-792-3307
Women/Men/Kids

Gucci
www.gucci.com
310-278-3451
Women/Men

Hermès
www.hermes.com
800-441-4488
Women/Men

Imitation of Christ
www.imitationofchrist.com
Women

J. Crew
www.jcrew.com
800-562-0258
Women/Men/Kids, accessories

Jack Taylor
310-274-7276
Men

Jimmy Choo
www.jimmychoo.com
310-860-9045
212-593-0800
Women's shoes and accessories

Juicy Couture
www.juicycouture.com
At Saks Fifth Avenue, Barneys New
York, Neiman Marcus, Ron
Herman, and select retailers
nationwide
Women/Men/Kids

Kangol
www.kangol.com
212-724-1172
Hats

Lanvin
www.lanvin.com
Women

Levi's
www.levis.com
Women/Men/Kids

Libertine
johnsonhartig@aol.com
Select retailers nationwide
Women/Men

Louis Vuitton
www.louisvuitton.com
866-VUITTON
Women/Men

Manolo Blahnik
212-582-1583
Neiman Marcus, Bergdorf
Goodman, and select retailers
nationwide
Women's shoes

Marni
www.marni.com
323-782-1101
Women

Milk Fed
Select retailers nationwide
Women/Men/Kids

Miu Miu
www.miumiu.com
323-651-0072
Women

Mogg Jeans
www.moggjeans.com
323-860-MOGG
Women/Men

Oscar de la Renta
www.oscardelarenta.com
Select retailers nationwide
Women

Peter Som
www.petersom.com
212-221-5991
Women

Prada
www.prada.com
323-782-0202; 212-327-4200
Women/Men

Rick Owens
www.net-a-porter.com
Select retailers nationwide
Women/Men

Tracey Ross
www.traceyross.com
8595 Sunset Blvd.
Los Angeles, CA
310-854-1996
*Women/Kids, shoes, accessories,
books*

Tree
323-460-6398
Women

True Religion Jeans
www.truereligionbrandjeans.com
323-325-9821
Women/Men

Vans
www.vans.com
800-826-7800
Shoes